Also by Kim D. H. Butler:

Live Your Life Insurance: Surprising Strategies to Build Lifelong Prosperity with Your Whole Life Policy
(Available on Amazon.com or LiveYourLifeInsurance.com)

Busting the Financial Planning Lies: Learn to Use Prosperity Economics to Build Sustainable Wealth
(Available on Amazon.com or ProsperityPeaks.com)

Busting the Retirement Lies: Living with Passion, Purpose, and Abundance Throughout Our Lives
(Available on Amazon.com or ProsperityPeaks.com)

Financial Planning Has Failed: Reject Typical Financial Advice and Create Sustainable Wealth—Without Wall Street Risks!
(Our gift to you in appreciation of your purchase of this book, you can download this book for free at ProsperityPeaks.com / Financial)

Look for these forthcoming books from Kim Butler and the Prosperity Economics Movement:

Busting the Mutual Fund Lies

Busting the Life Insurance Lies

Praise for *Busting the Interest Rate Lies*

"Amazing proof about 30 year mortgages being more effective than 15 year mortgages."

Tim Barnett
President, America's Mortgage Center, Ltd.

"Kim's newest book contains a great story on using using life insurance and investment real estate together."

Tom Dyson
Publisher, Palm Beach Research Group

"Busting the Interest Rate Lies provides an interesting and helpful view on taxes."

Warren Taryle, CPA, MST
Taryle Accounting, PLLC

"Investment education, some for the masses, some for the millionaires."

Todd Strobel
"No BS Money Guy"

"Great practical strategies! Anyone who wants to know how interest rates really work should read this book. Check out the car-buying section that shows why 'zero-percent financing' doesn't cost zero percent."

Babs Smith,
Owner and CEO, Strategic Coach Inc.

"This is a must-have book in every household in America. Getting your best negotiated price on a purchase of automobiles, equipment, rental properties, personal residence, and paying for education is only a small piece of the cost. This book is a major piece to your purchasing decisions!"

Tim Cooper, CRFA
Ripple Effect Investment Strategies, LLC

Busting the Interest Rate Lies

*Discover the Whole Truth About Money
and How You Can Keep Control of Yours*

KIM D. H. BUTLER

with Mona Kuljurgis

PROSPERITY ECONOMICS MOVEMENT

Busting the Interest Rate Lies
Copyright © 2016 Kim D. H. Butler

ISBN: 978-0-9913054-1-4

First Print Edition
March 2016

Produced in the United States of America

Prosperity Economics Movement
22790 Highway 259 South
Mount Enterprise, TX 75681
www.ProsperityPeaks.com

This book was published with the guidance and services of Social Motion Publishing, a benefit corporation that specializes in social-impact books. For more information, go to www.SocialMotionPublishing.com.

Contents

Preface

This is a short book that tells the story of a life lived with interest—the kind you pay and the kind you earn. Its goal is to open your eyes to the *whole truth* surrounding the many facets of interest that you'll encounter, and have encountered, throughout your life. Simply put, interest is unavoidable, whether paid or earned, in our modern society—and yet, the vast majority of people don't truly understand it well enough.

Unfortunately, there are many "interest rate lies" within the marketing messages and financial advice we receive almost daily, lies that have the single purpose of separating you from your hard-earned money—either leading you to pay more than you should or earn less than you could. And this won't go away, because the major media are heavily influenced by financial-institution advertisers and publicity, and the financial institutions themselves have a vested interest in maximizing their earnings from your money. So, next time you're watching a cable-TV finance show that includes someone glowing about the stock market, and in the next commercial break you see an ad from a mutual fund company, ask yourself

x Busting the Interest Rate Lies

how there might just be a connection. It isn't a conspiracy as much as it is a matter of simple influence—if someone had you write a news piece about your boss that would air on national TV, I'll make a bet that you'd probably be favorable toward this person who's issuing your paycheck.

As my financial advisory practice grew over the past couple decades, I learned that I wanted to do things differently. While yes, we make some of our money from financial products, we fundamentally operate with fiduciary responsibility toward our clients— in plain terms this means if it's not right for our client, we don't recommend it, even if it would make us more money. But beyond that, I wanted us to practice and promote the "whole truth" about financial planning, a concept I named *Prosperity Economics*. Due to mass media and mass marketing, both of which cater to the lowest common denominator, financial planning for most people has come to mean "investing in the stock market." We feel this is very misleading and, in too many cases, premature. The first financial concept we feel every person should understand is interest, because it is a vital part of everyone's financial picture—and yet, far too many "financial planners" don't address it.

Lastly, one of the 7 Principles of Prosperity that we teach is *Control*. (Read about all seven principles in our ebook, *Financial Planning Has Failed*, which you can download for free at ProsperityPeaks.com/financial.) As with many things in life, it's wiser and healthier to focus on what you have control over, whether it be thoughts, beliefs, or actions. This includes how you handle interest (again, paid and earned) in your finances. So, while you don't have control over interest rates, you do have control over how you handle them. And this begins with understanding how they function in the course of your purchases, savings, and investments, which we illustrate through this story.

I trust you'll find the material in *Busting the Interest Rate Lies* educational and a fun read. Likewise, I hope you'll think of someone who could benefit from the information with whom you'll share this book. Perhaps, you'll even go as far as starting a discussion group around these topics. Whatever the case, if you discover you or someone you know would like personalized assistance, please see the Prosperity Economics Advisor who recommended this book or reach out to us through ProsperityPeaks.com—home of The Prosperity Economics Movement.

Kim D. H. Butler
Mt. Enterprise, TX
January 2016

Introduction

Finance and retirement. They are the topics of many news broadcasts and TV shows, in fact entire cable networks are devoted to them. I even devoted a great deal of time in my previous books, *Busting the Retirement Lies* and *Busting the Financial Planning Lies,* to the subjects. But upon further reflection, I may have been too quick to write those books before this one.

Because before we can talk about saving, before we can even talk about financial strategies, we have to talk interest rates.

So much of the hype out there is pretty advanced: there are brokers screaming and quacking about which stocks to buy, analysts droning on about the next corporate merger, and advertising squawking about the next great financing deal. Amidst it all, we often feel embarrassed or intimidated to ask the most basic questions—questions that were never addressed at home, in school, or any other formal outlet.

This wicked combination of educational neglect and biased, overly sophisticated hype makes for a population ripe for the taking. And taken we have been.

Leading up to the financial crisis of 2008, thousands upon thousands signed on to massive mortgage loans their moderate incomes couldn't sustain. With adjustable-rate mortgages (ARMs) instead of fixed ones, interest rates skyrocketed after an artificially low introductory teaser period. With the end of this introductory period came the end of low monthly payments. And with the end of low monthly payments came the mortgage defaults. The results are now legendary—foreclosure, foreclosure, foreclosure.

As the banks responsible for these "sub-prime" mortgages watched tens of thousands of these loans default, the homes that secured them plummeted in price. As a result, the banks themselves began to collapse. Consequently, the businesses that relied on the banks, and the folks they employed, faltered. Companies downsized and laid off workers. The result was the second wave of this economic disaster with the same result—foreclosure, foreclosure, foreclosure.

Business revenue dwindled, stock values plummeted, retirement savings lost, jobs cut, and homes abandoned, all for the lack of one thing—a rudimentary understanding of interest rates.

Will this ever happen again? In some way, shape, or form, almost certainly. While the events of 2008 were unprecedented in their scope and severity, recessions happen. And on a personal level, economic downturns are a prospect for all of us at almost any given time with the sudden loss of a job, diagnosis of a serious medical condition, and other unpredictable turns. What counts the most is focusing on what you *can* control—which, in the scope of this book, means understanding how interest rates affect your financial health and wellbeing.

This starts with busting what is perhaps the ultimate interest rate lie: The consequences of borrowing money can be sidestepped by complicated loan terms, low monthly payments, and long repayment periods. It's a concept that doesn't work for cars, for homes, for credit cards, for student loans, or for any other reason to borrow money that exists in this credit-crazed day and age. Once you see through the haze of imposed confusion, you will see how fundamentally interest "giveth and taketh away." And as we proceed through this book, we'll show you where to make smarter choices so that interest works in your favor.

For our journey, we only need two teaching tools—Truth Concepts software, a financial application used by Prosperity Economics Advisors to reveal the whole truth about money, and fictional narrative.

We are using fictional narrative because it's a good way to illustrate sometimes complex and dry material, and we are using Truth Concepts (TruthConcepts.com) because of its clarity, sophistication, and ease of use. If you are not ready to dive into this software just yet, you can just follow along with the screenshots we've included or use any of the myriad online financial calculators for the basics. And you can always contact one of our Prosperity Economics Advisors for help with crunching the numbers for your specific situation.

Ready? All right. Let's meet our characters, Gary and Emily.* Gary's in his final year of high school when Emily visits his graduating class as a Prosperity Economics Advisor to explain the simple math of interest rates and their often daunting applications—applications that apply to anyone who will borrow, save, or invest their money. And in the civilized world, that's everyone.

---

* Our two characters are fictional and represent composites of many clients and Prosperity Economics Advisors.

CHAPTER 1

Don't Pay Interest... Earn It

Gary walked down the hall to his fifth-period class. He remembered that today was going to be a guest speaker, and he was looking forward to a break from the usual. He liked fifth period because it was math class, and Gary was pretty good at math. Ms. Johnson was quick and funny, her delivery clear and straightforward. It was remedial math, which Gary didn't quite understand being in because he was good at math and was doing well in this class. Still, he went with the program, so here he was.

Today was bright and sunny, and the windows were open to the warm, breezy air outside. It was May, and soon his last days of high school would be behind him. The beloved Ms. Johnson was sitting behind her desk as usual. She'd been his math teacher three years in a row, now. Somehow, he thought he would miss her.

Next to her stood a woman he didn't recognize. She seemed overly dressed for high school, so Gary assumed this was the guest speaker. She and Ms. Johnson leaned over some papers on the desk and talked quietly. On the board was written, *Prosperity Economics*.

The guest speaker came to the front of the room. Ms. Johnson stood up and spoke from behind her desk.

"Ladies and gentleman, this is Emily Peterson. She's a financial advisor in town. More specifically, she's a Prosperity Economics Advisor."

The speaker and Ms. Johnson smiled at each other.

"She's going to talk to you about *why* we are doing all this math in the first place, well, at least the main reason. If it were up to me, we would have a full year of this information, but unfortunately, it's not up to me — yet — so we're only going to have one day.

"This is where the rubber hits the road, people. This is what all this math is about. Some of you will have other reasons to apply basic math, you will use it to build and measure, to plan and schedule, but all of you — *all of you* — will use it for the purposes Emily is about to discuss. All of you will use it to track money. And I suggest you get your heads around it right away, because it's going to make a huge difference in your life, at every stage in life.

"And there are forces that will try to part you from your money at every turn, so pay attention. What Emily is about to say is going to change the course of your life, if you're smart enough to let it."

Emily came to the front of the class. She stood in front of a huge flat-screen monitor at the front of the room connected to a laptop and commanded the laptop's remote.

"Thank you, Ms. Johnson. I appreciate you having me here," said Emily. She then looked to the students. "I'm going to talk about something I wished someone had talked to me about when I was in high school. For all the algebra, and literature, chemistry and history they talk about in here, they don't talk about the one thing all of you, I mean *all* of you, will have to deal with the moment you step out of these doors, and for every minute for the rest of your life — money.

"Perhaps some of you have plans to live off the land and forage for food, but for the rest of you, you'll have to deal with money.

"By the way, I have a master's degree in Greek literature from a prestigious university. Couldn't make any money with that—who'd've thunk it?—and I just recently paid off my gargantuan student loans. So, in the interest of full disclosure...

"I became a Prosperity Economics financial advisor when I realized I was in the pits of financial dispair. Waiting tables wouldn't cover the bills anymore, especially when my student loan payments became due, and teaching was less financially rewarding than waiting tables.

"Yes. Did you hear me? I made *less* money teaching part-time than as a waitress— a word to the wise.

"So, financial advising it is. And here I am.

"What happened to me will happen to many of you. You will go on to college. You will get many student loans and credit cards to pay for college because they will offer them to you; they will barrage you with these offers, in fact.

"You will take them because none of these entities, either the student loan lenders or the credit card companies, will tell you the dire consequences of incurring so much debt at the beginning of your life. They will not tell you this because it will benefit them to have you beholden to them. They will make a whole lot of money off of you.

"You will get a college degree and then a job, and then you will wonder, *when does the freedom part come?* Because remember when everyone said, 'once you get out of high school, then you'll be free'. Or remember when they said, 'just get your degree, then you'll be free.'

"And you did everything everybody said, but you look at

your balance sheet now and think, *freedom! I will never be free of this $50,000 of student loan debt and this $10,000 worth of credit card debt. With my entry-level job and my living expenses, I will be beholden to these financial companies for the rest of my life.*

"And the financial companies will smile. They will rub their hands together, tell themselves 'good job,' and smile.

"Just sayin'."

Ms. Emily Peterson had everyone's attention. Some looked horrified, but she had everyone's attention.

She flicked on the flat screen monitor. Up came a slide:

prosperityeconomicsmovement

Prosperity Economics shows us how to optimize wealth by keeping it in our control rather than delegating our financial futures to Wall Street, big corporations, and the government.

"Right now I'd like to talk about Rocket Ismail's story. Rocket Ismail was the NFL's #1 draft pick in 1991. He signed an $18.8 million guaranteed 4-year contract, the richest contract in NFL history at the time, and played ten years of pro football. After his decade-long career, according to a 2009 *Sports Illustrated* article, he was broke.

"In fact, according to the same article, 78 percent of professional NFL football players are broke or close to broke two years after their football careers end. They earn tens of millions of dollars, retire from football at 35 years old, and go broke 24 months later. The same goes for sixty percent of NBA basketball players only five years after retirement.

"Imagine 78 percent of all your favorite football players. That's the vast majority.

"In contrast, let's look at Theodore R. Johnson. He worked for UPS for 29 years, never exceeding a $14,000 per year salary. Before he died in 1991, his net worth was estimated at $70 million, and he consequently created a $24 million scholarship foundation.

"How did he do it? Savings and investing, conscientiously and diligently, for the whole of his life.

"Why do I say this? Because money is important. I want you to listen. Some of you will make or manage a lot of money, and you will always have creditors at your door. Others of you will earn modest incomes, build savings, and sleep soundly at night.

"I want you to be among the ones who sleep soundly, and what I'm about to tell you could make that difference.

"Repeat after me: A fool and his money are soon parted."

The class repeated after her: "A fool and his money are soon parted."

"Excellent. Thank you. Okay. Let's begin."

Ms. Peterson clicked her remote and a chart came up on the flat screen.

"Simple math," she said. "That's what we're dealing with. Just simple math. You learned it in eighth grade, and again in Ms. Johnson's class. Money is based on simple math: addition, subtraction, multiplication, division, and most importantly, percentages.

"So, let's talk about interest rates.

"This is the stuff you'll pay when you're a debtor and earn

when you're a saver or investor.

"Remember, we want to *earn* this stuff, not *owe* it. Repeat after me: *we want to earn this stuff, not owe it.*"

The class laughed and repeated her words.

"Excellent. And it's all just percentages, my friends. Basic math expressed as percentages."

The room was quiet and Ms. Peterson clicked to another chart.

"Now, what's your name?" She pointed straight at Gary, and Gary told her his name.

"Great. Gary. Now, if Gary gave me $100 to invest, and I paid him *simple* interest of 5% per year, Gary would earn $5 after the first year, giving him a total of $105. After the second year, he would earn another $5, giving him a total of $110. After the third year, another $5, giving him a total of $115.

"Simple interest is earned on the principal only, the original $100 Gary gave me. When it's calculated, it does not factor in any interest paid.

"So, for as long as I held the $100 for Gary, he would earn five dollars in interest every year, no more, no less. Even as his account grew to, say, $150 over 10 years ($5 interest × 10 years = $50 in interest), it would still only earn him $5 per year.

"Again, this is because simple interest is calculated on principal only. Whatever interest Gary earns in the present does *not* affect the interest he earns in the future. If Gary leaves his $100 with me untouched, he will only get five dollars in interest every year, regardless of how much interest he accumulates on that $100 over time.

"In the real world, simple interest is used far less than compound interest, but it's important to discuss it to understand the difference."

Ms. Peterson clicked to another slide.

"Now let's talk about compound interest. Compound interest is different than simple interest because whatever accrues on Gary's $100 in the present *factors into* the interest that accrues in the future.

"In other words, with compound interest, the interest you earn over time *does* impact the interest you earn in the future — thus the name, 'compounding.'

"So if Gary gives me $100 and I pay him 5% per year *compounding* interest, after one year I'll owe Gary $5 in interest. His total account balance will be $105. This, however, is where the similarities between the two methods end.

"The second year, I'll have to pay Gary 5% interest on his new balance of $105, not just his original $100 deposit.

"Therefore, my interest payment in year two will be 5% of the $105, equaling $5.25. This gives Gary $110.25 after two years. In year three, I'll have to base my 5% interest payment on his new $110.25 balance, which will equal $5.51. This brings his total to $115.76 in three years.

The class was quiet.

"I know what you're thinking," said Emily Peterson. "You're thinking, *ooooooooooohh, 76 more cents. How exciting. That's not much difference at all. Why should I care about the difference between compound and simple interest?*

"You should care for this:

"Imagine compounding interest over millions of people —not just for $100, but for thousands, tens of thousands, hundreds of thousands, and more. And imagine that interest compounding over 10, 20, 30, and 50 years.

"That's where the money comes in. That's how banks get rich, and people lose their shirts, and the world keeps turning.

"Here's a quick pop quiz to show the power of compound interest. Which would you rather have, a million dollars or a penny that doubles every day for 30 days?"

The classmates looked at each other as a boy wondered aloud, "Is this a trick question?"

After a moment, a girl in the front row gave the seemingly obvious answer. "I'll take the million dollars, please!"

"Most people would," said Emily. "And then they're surprised to learn that the doubling penny would have given them more than five million dollars in 30 days!"

Now heads were shaking in disbelief.

"Here, let me show you," Emily offered as she clicked to the next slide. Sure enough, the numbers were there in black and white:

Day 1: $.01	Day 11: $10.24	Day 21: $10,485.76
Day 2: $.02	Day 12: $20.48	Day 22: $20,971.52
Day 3: $.04	Day 13: $40.96	Day 23: $41,943.04
Day 4: $.08	Day 14: $81.92	Day 24: $83,886.08
Day 5: $.16	Day 15: $163.84	Day 25: $167,772.16
Day 6: $.32	Day 16: $327.68	Day 26: $335,544.32
Day 7: $.64	Day 17: $655.36	Day 27: $671,088.64
Day 8: $1.28	Day 18: $1,310.72	Day 28: $1,342,177.28
Day 9: $2.56	Day 19: $2,621.44	Day 29: $2,684,354.56
Day 10: $5.12	Day 20: $5,242.88	Day 30: $5,368,709.12

"That's pretty amazing... I never would've guessed!" exclaimed one student. Emily seemed pleased.

"Now let me ask you another question," mused the guest speaker who now had the room's full attention. "Would you rather *owe* a million dollars, or a penny doubled each day?"

"Well, now I'll pick the million dollars for sure," said the redhead in the front row who had answered before. "Or neither!"

"Good idea," chuckled Emily. "And perhaps the example of a doubling penny shows how easy it is to underestimate the power of interest rates, whether you're saving or borrowing. Remember, kids, you want to earn interest, not pay it. Repeat after me."

"We want to earn interest, not pay it." Everyone laughed.

"So how do we do that?" someone shouted.

"I'm so glad you asked!" Ms. Peterson yelled back. "Excellent question."

She clicked over to another slide.

"It's by saving and investing.

"Remember Mr. Theodore R. Johnson? He built his $70 million fortune by saving 20% of his $14,000 income from United Parcel Service. He saved 20% of his income year in and year out, every single year.

"Now you may be thinking, *20%!?!? That doesn't sound like much. I can put aside 20%.* But, believe me, when the advertisers tighten their grip on you, you'll begin to think you actually *need* a newer car, a bigger house, a better smart phone, and more designer clothes. You'll believe the measure of your worth depends on it. And then the Joneses come along, and you start feeling like you need to keep up with them. Then you'll think, *20%! I need that money to pay the interest on my brand-new car and my monolithic house payment. I can't afford to set that aside in a savings or investment account.*

"It will be a pity, and it will be sad. Try not to let the advertisers wrap their steel grip around you, if they haven't already, which is unlikely.

"If you can resist that steel grip, you'll save yourself a lot of pain and heartache."

You could hear a pin drop in the room.

"So, let's get back down to business."

Emily waved her hand and clicked through to another slide.

"Now what is the difference between saving and investing? The two terms are used interchangeably, but for our purposes, we'll talk about savings as something you do for the short-term. You save for a car, a vacation, or an emergency. Money in savings needs to be accessed immediately - and be completely safe. When your daughter's medical bills come due or your roof needs replacing, you need to dig into that money easily, and you need to be assured it's there in full. You can't take any chances that it was lost in a stock market dive or wiped out in a real estate deal.

"That's why most people put their savings, especially their emergency fund savings, in a savings account at the bank. This money can be accessed not only by a simple trip to a branch or ATM machine, it is also insured by the Federal Deposit Insurance Corporation, the FDIC, a government agency backed by taxpayers that guarantees each depositors' money for up to, currently, $250,000.

"That means that if a bank fails, as so many did in 2008, depositors are guaranteed to get their money back."

"Wouldn't you want all of your money to be insured?" yelled someone from the back of the room.

"Yes. You would," said Emily. "But there's a cost to all that safety.

"Today, savings accounts earn an annual compound interest rate of less than 1%. That's a tiny return, even for large amounts of money."

"How come you used 5% in earlier examples?" asked someone sort of at the same time they raised their hand.

"Well, I used the 5% return because that's what money can

earn in a cash value whole life insurance policy right now in 2015. Cash value whole life is another type of savings vehicle, something people use after they've built a healthy emergency fund. Once your savings account is squared away, people often continue saving, earning interest at a higher rate, with a cash value whole life policy. But, that's for another time. Right now we're talking about savings accounts, so let's stick to that.

"So, as you can see, saving is an imperative part of your financial future, whether it's in a savings account or a cash value whole life policy."

"So, how is that different from investing?" asked a girl in the front row.

"Well," said Emily, "investing is often for the long term. It's money you set aside to live off of later in life. When you invest, you typically don't do that in a savings account or cash value whole life policy. You rather invest in the stock market, real estate, or in businesses. Investments are more difficult to access than savings, more difficult to cash out of, so to speak. There are fees, penalties, and some investments, like real estate, need to be sold before you can get your money out.

"In addition, investments are typically *not* insured. The FDIC will not come to your rescue if your stocks drop in value or the real estate market crashes. Unlike a savings account that pays less than 1% per year though, investments can pay 8%, 9%, 10% per year and more. But know this: investments can also bottom out. They can lose 8%, 9%, 10% and more, if you are unlucky or not careful. In fact, they can lose your entire balance; they can lose everything.

The class was silent.

"My entire point in saying this is for one reason, and one reason only: You need both. You need both savings and investments in your life. Repeat after me.

"You need both savings and investments in your life," the entire class chimed.

"Excellent. Good," Emily continued.

"Listen, people, from the moment you walk out of this high school, forces will converge to try to separate you from your money. They will tell you your value as a person depends on it, they will tell you your boyfriend or girlfriend will stay with you because of it, they will tell you your very life may depend on it.

"Do me this favor. Don't let this class be the last of your financial education. Vow this. Vow right here and right now to read one book per year about money. Just one book. Only one. There are some excellent books published and recommended by the Prosperity Economics Movement. Those are a good place to start, but regardless of which book you choose, vow to read one every year. Let me hear it!"

The class repeated, "We vow to read one book per year about money."

"Thank you," she replied. "Now, since we're talking about parting you from your money, I'm going to talk about two rackets that will do their best at that as soon as you take your graduation caps off.

"Those two rackets are student loans and credit cards."

Emily clicked the remote to change slides. She had given this long introduction to get to this point. She wanted to make it emphatically.

"According to the Institute for College Access and Success, the average student loan debt for graduating college seniors in 2012 was $29,400. Imagine, almost $30,000 in debt, and you haven't even started out in life yet.

"In fact, according to a study by the Federal Reserve Bank of New

York, student loan debt has risen, in total, from $390 billion in 2005 to $966 billion in 2012 — it's more than doubled in only seven years.

"If your interest rate on that $29,400 of student loans is only a subsidized 6%, do you know what your monthly payments would be for a 10-year loan?"

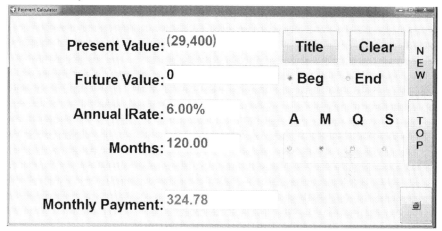

Figure 1

"I'm embarrassed to say that this was about the amount of student loan debt I graduated with. Did I tell you I have a master's in Greek literature? Yes, I do. Did I tell you I can make more money waiting tables than teaching Greek literature? Yes. I did. OK. Just checking.

"People, I hate to say this, but college is a racket. It's a business, like any other. People will say a college education is hallowed, sacred, and incorruptible. It is not.

"There are as many people looking to make a buck off of college students as any other demographic, and it starts with the college fees and tuition themselves.

"Here's how to combat that: Know the system. Go to financial aid workshops. Get as many grants and scholarships as you can before you start attending. Wait a few years to no longer be claimed as a dependent on your parents' tax return; in that way, your family's income will not be considered when applying for grants and scholarships, only your own.

"Don't be sucked in by the supposed cachet of prestigious 4-year universities. It might be fun to drop the name of a certain school, but you'll be paying for that name-dropping privilege for decades. Acquire your first two-years' credits at a community college — and then transfer. The university will still be there, your degree will bear its name, but you'll save yourself tens of thousands of dollars in the long run.

"Know that you can decline any loan or portion thereof they offer you. Nowhere in *my* student loan offer-letters did they mention that.

"When I called the financial aid office to ask about this, the women said, 'Just take a pen and cross out any amounts you don't want. Handwrite in the lowered amounts you *do* want, and send it back.'

"Gee. Thanks. Glad I asked. That seems much less official than I thought.

"I would later realize that that one phone call saved me thousands upon thousands of dollars I didn't have to repay later in life.

"And, lastly, know that student loan debt cannot be discharged in bankruptcy. Did you hear me…? This means filing for bankruptcy will not get rid of your student loans. So, again… student loans *cannot* be discharged in bankruptcy. In fact, repeat it after me."

"Student loans cannot be discharged in bankruptcy," the class repeated hesitantly.

"Good. Know that they will garnish your wages—garnish your wages—to get their money back. And there isn't a darn thing you can do about it.

"All of this is just to say that, though it feels like a long time from where you're sitting, four years of college goes by fast.

"Student loans that finance those years? They can last forever."

The class shifted uncomfortably. Someone in the second row raised their hand and asked, "Shouldn't they talk to us about this long before our last semester in high school?"

"Yes, they absolutely should," replied Emily. "I'm sorry they don't. But like I said, my friends, though it gives me no pleasure — it's a racket. So, that's one debt college students take on while they're in college; here's another.

"In 2013, the average college student graduated with $3000 worth of credit card debt. Now, that may pale in comparison to the massive student loan debt they accrue, but let's take a look at the kind of interest rates they pay.

"Remember when we talked about what banks pay to depositors in a savings account? About one percent per year. Do you know how much banks *charge* to lend money via credit cards? They charge 20 times that.

"If the bank is paying you 1 percent per year in a savings account, they may be charging you 20 percent per year to lend you money via a credit card.

"If you rack up $10,000 on your credit card, at a 20% interest rate, your monthly *minimum* payment would be about $163." [See Figure 2, next page.]

"But, if you want to pay that off in five years — FIVE years — you actually have to pay more like $260 per month. That's $260 a month every single month for 60 months." [See Figure 3, next page.]

"Think of that: 20%. It would be hard to get that in the most risky, volatile, and insecure investment. But credit companies charge it, year in and year out, to millions of ordinary people every day.

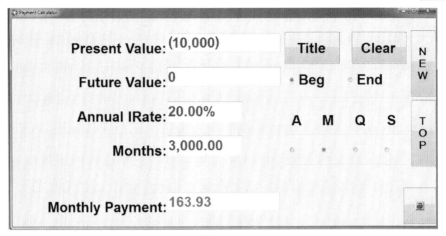

Figure 2

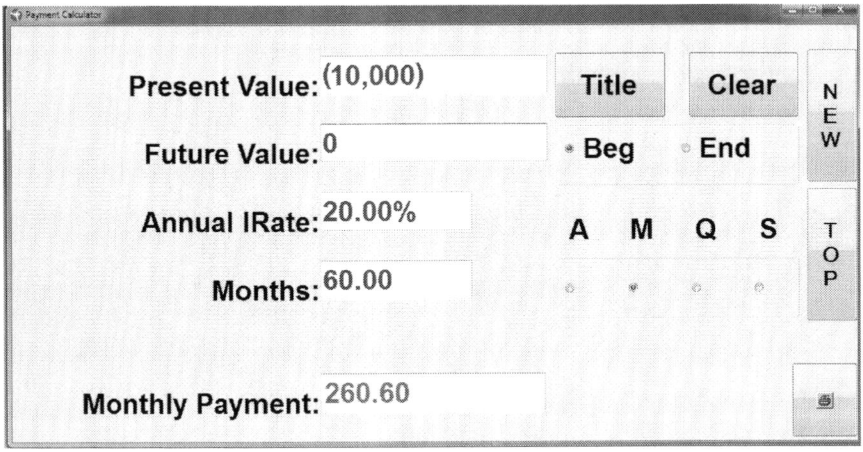

Figure 3

"Now let me tell you a story. Elizabeth Warren is now a Senator from Massachusetts. In 2006 she was a Harvard law professor studying consumer finance. In the James D. Scurlock documentary of that same year, *Maxed Out*, Warren relays a story about a lecture she gave to some high-level bank executives. At the lecture, she explained that, according to her research, if the executives would stop issuing credit to their least credit-worthy customers, specifically those that had recently declared bankruptcy, they could significantly decrease their defaults.

"Warren says that an executive at the back of the room interrupted. He was one of the big shots because the whole room went quiet. This executive retorted that if the bank eliminated the least credit-worthy customers from their roles, the bank would lose a lot of profit.

"Warren asked why.

"The executive answered that the bank *made all their money off their least credit-worthy customers.* He explained that people who declared bankruptcy can't declare it again for a decade, have developed a taste for credit, and are willing to make minimum monthly payments…sometimes forever. In other words, the bank can bleed them dry.

"I have a newsflash for you," Emily whispered, sounding very serious, "those least credit-worthy customers… are you."

She let that reality fall on the students for a moment before continuing.

"College students have the least experience with financial literacy and discipline. That's why the credit card companies, and even the student loan corporations, go after them with such a vengeance.

"Before the Credit Card Act of 2009, banks would barrage college campuses with credit card sign-up tables, offer free mugs, Frisbees, and ten-thousand-dollars worth of credit to an 18-year-old with a bookstore job. They would give just over two-weeks notice before increasing interest rates. And they would even "double-bill," charging interest on current charges *and* previous charges, even if the previous ones had already been paid off.

"The 2009 law puts an end to these practices, but that doesn't make these companies any less aggressive. A 2012 study in the

International Journal of Business and Social Science said that college students, whether employed and with a credit history or not, were solicited for credit cards between 25-50 times per year.

"So, don't be duped by these financial predators. Having a boatload of debt is *no way* to start out your life. Credit card and student loan corporations prey on the weak, the undisciplined, and the uninformed. Don't be one of them."

There was silence in the room. You could feel the air shift around the 17- and 18-year-olds as they contemplated their last few weeks of childhood.

One girl in the front row raised her hand, "But what if you already know someone who's in credit card trouble? What if this kind of information never got to them soon enough?"

"If someone's already in trouble, first they should stop taking on any new debt. No cash advances, new cards, new loans, nada. They must live within their means, or increase their income, even if it means big lifestyle changes! Otherwise they are just digging a deeper hole.

"Next, they should create a spending plan or budget—and see where they can find 'hidden money' to pay off debt faster. There are great tools to help, too, like Mint.com's software or the YNAB (You Need A Budget) system.

"Finally, if they aren't in a financial position to get the debts paid back within a few years, they should contact their creditors and ask for help. See if they will negotiate balances or interest rates. Oftentimes, creditors will only help those who are already behind on payments, but whether someone has defaulted on their payments or not, it may be possible to find a win-win solution."

The bell rang, but everyone stayed in their seats. Ms. Johnson made no move to dismiss the class.

"Look, guys," Emily added, "since you're in your last few weeks of high school, there's a good chance I may never see you again. And since I may never see you again, I'm going to tell you this.

"Life is about building. Ten percent of your life will be windfall, a stroke of good fortune, a win of the lottery. Another ten percent will be the floor dropping out from beneath you, a diagnosis, a crash and burn, a blow to the head.

"But 80 percent, the vast majority, will be you just building, brick by brick, stone by stone, a life that you desire, that you imagine, that you are proud of. Let it be *your* life, not someone else's. Money is important, even if you spend most of your life volunteering in the third-world or pursuing a life of uncompromising art. In fact, in the service of those causes, money is even more important. It will play a role in every part of your life.

Emily paused for a moment and looked around at the kids sitting at the threshold of adulthood and all it entails. She felt a pang of affection and empathy. She couldn't download her knowledge and experience to them. They'd have to walk their own paths in whatever lay ahead for themselves.

"Now, remember," Emily concluded, "you promised me. One book on money a year. No time like the present to get started."

There was a smattering of applause, some laughter, some thank-yous, and few people began gathering their bags. A group of students approached Emily at the front of the room.

Gary flipped through his notes and wrote down Emily's name at the top of the page. He thought for a moment, smiled at Ms. Johnson, then walked out the door.

CHAPTER 2

Cars: Drive Away with Savings

Gary's part-time job working for Vaipanzo Brothers construction during high school turned full-time after graduation. In his junior year, Gary began with the Vaipanzo's moving bricks from pile to pile. But, as time went on, the brothers placed more trust in Gary, and gave him more responsibility.

College was a possibility for Gary, and a lot of the kids from his school did go, but it wasn't a path for him. Unlike many of his class-mates, people relied on Gary from the start — his mother, sister, and aunt all depended on Gary to contribute. And Gary was bound and determined to do so. Of sound mind and strong body, Gary saw no reason why he couldn't make his way in the world, and help others along theirs as well.

The Vaipanzo's saw this. Though not a fuzzy bunch, they were fair, straightforward, and even generous with people who did well for them. Several years after his first day on the job, Gary counted himself among those they trusted. Starting out as a part-time apprentice in high school, by the time he was 28 years old, Gary had worked his way up to assistant superintendant.

And that same year, the Vaipanzo Brothers did very well. Along with his holiday bonus, a tradition at the company, this year the brothers began a profit-sharing program. And Gary had helped to run the most profitable job in the bunch. He imagined he might get a big check, but until the moment he unsealed the envelope, he didn't suspect how big.

He steadied himself on the edge of the wall as he read the numbers — $15,000. Together with his already biggest holiday bonus ever, $5000, he was looking at more money than he'd ever seen in his life at once — $20,000.

He and his mother stared silently at the two checks in her kitchen.

"I can't quite believe it, Gary. I don't know what to say, really, or what to do with this money," said his mom. "I mean, we sort of have our expenses covered here, but this is extra. I don't know what to do with it — and I'm a little scared of it."

Gary was embarrassed to admit he sort of felt the same way. The $1000 and $2000 holiday bonuses had always been spent on Christmas, or car repairs, or to replenish the emergency fund he always dipped into, despite his best efforts. But this $20,000, this was real money. It was money he could blow into the wind if he wasn't careful.

His mother could practically read his mind.

"Gary, I can't advise you on what to do with this. Right now, we're good here. We had the roof replaced last year, and the water heater a few months ago. Use this money, sweetheart. Use it wisely, but use it for yourself."

Gary stood quietly for a long moment. This, this moment, was new to him, this feeling of abundance; it was a strange sensation. He squirmed in the discomfort.

"I don't know what to do with this, Mom. Maybe a new car? I've always wanted to drive a brand new car. How about that Chevy—"

And just then, a box clattered to the floor. Cleaning out his old room, Gary's mom uncovered a box of his old texts and notes from high school, a box that sat perched on the corner of the kitchen table, until now. Splattered across the kitchen floor were books and papers, with one notebook, open to a middle page, splayed across the top of the pile. Scrawled in all capital letters near the top of the page was the word, *MONEY*, and directly below that, the name, Emily Peterson.

After a long silence, Gary and his mom finally raised their eyes to look up at each other.

"Um, do you want to call this Emily Peterson?" muttered his mom.

"Uh, yeah, sure. Why don't I do that," replied Gary.

Slowly, they both picked up the books and papers and began loading them back again into the box. Gary tucked the notebook with Emily's name under his arm.

Neither of them ever spoke of that moment again.

* * * * * * * *

Emily Peterson was in the same office building she occupied a decade ago, but had now upgraded to a bigger space. She remembered that visit to Gary's high school and was happy and surprised to see a student from almost a decade earlier.

"Hello Gary. It's nice to see you. What a surprise, after all this time."

"Thanks, Emily. Nice to see you too. Yes, I didn't think I'd have much reason in my life to visit a financial advisor, but funny things happen."

"I'm glad funny things happen, Gary. Tell me what's going on."

Gary told Emily about the $20,000 bonus and profit-sharing check, about the box spilling to the kitchen floor, and about his plan to use his money to buy a new car. He also said that $20,000 was the most money he'd ever seen at once in his life.

"It's an honor that you came to see me, Gary. And I'm impressed with your diligence and deliberateness. Most people would have blown that money in a month—it's unusual for folks to own up to a blind side. Your year-end bonuses are a lot of money, and you're right to want to allocate it thoughtfully."

"Thanks, Emily, but I'm hoping part of that allocation includes a new car. I've been looking at some nice ones, and I'm really looking forward to retiring my old hand-me-down."

"All right, Gary, that's a possibility, but before we talk about cars, let's talk about something else—a concept I introduce all of my clients to. It pertains to cars, but it can really be applied to any decision. Let's run it with your impending car purchase in mind."

"Sure," Gary responded.

"OK, excellent. What I'd like to discuss," Emily went on, "is the difference between accounting costs and opportunity costs." She took out a piece of paper and wrote across it in big black marker:

Accounting Cost + Opportunity Costs = Economic Cost

Gary leaned over the desk to see the paper more clearly. "That sounds familiar," he said, "We may have talked about this in Ms. Johnson's class."

"I wouldn't doubt it," said Emily, "Ms. Johnson's an excellent teacher. Okay, let me explain the difference. Very simply, accounting costs are literal; they're the number on the price tag, the dollar figure on the invoice, the amount charged at the register when making your purchase. In our car purchasing scenario, it'd be the actual price of the car you buy."

"Okay. I'm with you so far," said Gary.

"Excellent. So, opportunity costs are much more theoretical, and they can sometimes be difficult to assess. In an Economics 101 class, opportunity cost is defined as the value of the *next best* alternative foregone when making a decision. It's the option you *give up*, the next best option, when deciding on what you believe is the best choice."

"Yes," said Gary. "I remember it from Ms. Johnson's class."

"Good. I'm a Prosperity Economics advisor, Gary, and as I always say, I love to tell the whole truth about money. So, because of this, let's measure not only the *accounting costs* of car buying, but the *opportunity costs* as well."

"Okay."

"And let's measure these costs over 50 years, a car-buying lifetime." Emily began tapping on her keyboard and turned her monitor towards Gary. "This is Truth Concepts software—a financial calculator that many Prosperity Economics Advisors use. I'm going to use it now to run *opportunity* and *accounting* costs for several car-purchasing scenarios. Sound good?"

"Sounds good to me."

"What I'm pulling up right now is the Automobile Purchase Calculator. Now, remember, we're running this for a car-buying lifetime, approximately 50 years. Like you, our sample car buyer is paying cash for her cars — pulling it out of her savings account — where she manages to save $10,000 per year."

"Okay," Gary said.

"$10,000 per year," Emily continued, "saved over 50 years—*without* accruing any interest—is $500,000. If we add only a 1-percent interest rate to this account, let's see what we get."

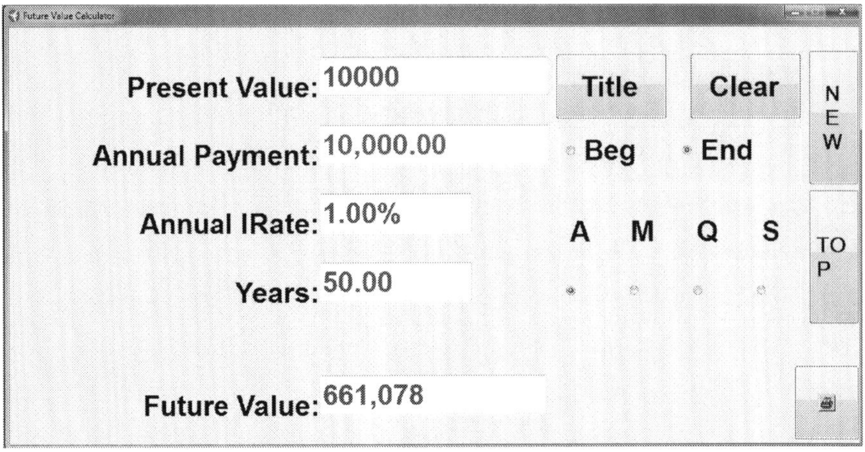

Figure 4

"$661,078. That's a lot of money!" said Gary

"Yep. But we're pulling out money from this account to buy cars, right? So, let's see what happens when we factor that in."

Emily pulled up a different calculator in the Truth Concepts software, one that analyzes auto purchases.

"Let's run *economic* costs—*accounting* costs plus *opportunity* costs—for three scenarios. In scenario one, our car buyer will buy a new $50,000 car every five years. In scenario two, she'll buy a $25,000 late-model used car every five years. And, in scenario three, she'll buy an earlier-model $15,000 used car every five years."

She tapped away on her keyboard as Gary mentally caught up. Then she continued explaining the concept.

"Those numbers, as we discussed, are the *accounting* costs. As for the *opportunity* costs, we'll consider what the principal and interest *could* have grown to, had she left the money alone in the account over 50 years, without withdrawing anything for cars. So, let's run buying a $50,000 car every five years, first."

Emily showed Gary the screen shown in Figure 5.

Automobile Purchases

Current Value of Assets:	10,000		Auto Purchase Frequency:	5		
Annual Savings:	10,000.00		Actual Purchase Price:	50,000.00		
Annual Savings Increase (%):	0.00%		Ann. Auto Price Increase (%):	3.00%		
Net ROR on Savings (%):	5.00%		Sales Tax Rate (%):	0.00%		
Number of Years:	50		Ann. Auto Insurance	0.00		
Year of 1st Purchase:	5		Ann. Insurance Increase (%):	5		

Future Asset Val. WITHOUT Autos: 2,312,828
Cumulative Auto Costs: (1,195,617)
Actual Asset Val. WITH Auto Costs: (1,264,362)
True Cost Of Automobiles: (3,577,190)

Title   Clear   N E W

Yr	Annual Savings	EOY Asset Value NO Auto Costs	Automobile Purchase	Sales Tax	Cumulative Auto Costs	EOY Asset Value WITH Auto Costs	Loss of Future Asset Value
1	10,000	21,000				21,000	
2	10,000	32,550				32,550	
3	10,000	44,678				44,678	
4	10,000	57,411				57,411	
5	10,000	70,782	(56,275)		(56,275)	11,693	(59,089)
6	10,000	84,821			(56,275)	22,777	(62,044)
7	10,000	99,562			(56,275)	34,416	(65,146)
8	10,000	115,040			(56,275)	46,637	(68,403)
9	10,000	131,292			(56,275)	59,469	(71,823)
10	10,000	148,357	(65,239)		(121,514)	4,442	(143,915)
11	10,000	166,275			(121,514)	15,164	(151,111)
12	10,000	185,088			(121,514)	26,422	(158,666)
13	10,000	204,843			(121,514)	38,243	(166,600)
14	10,000	225,585			(121,514)	50,655	(174,930)
15	10,000	247,364	(75,629)		(197,144)	(15,723)	(263,087)
16	10,000	270,232			(197,144)	(6,009)	(276,241)
17	10,000	294,244			(197,144)	4,190	(290,054)
18	10,000	319,456			(197,144)	14,900	(304,556)
19	10,000	345,929			(197,144)	26,145	(319,784)
20	10,000	373,725	(87,675)		(284,819)	(54,107)	(427,832)
21	10,000	402,912			(284,819)	(46,312)	(449,224)
22	10,000	433,557			(284,819)	(38,128)	(471,685)
23	10,000	465,735			(284,819)	(29,534)	(495,269)

Figure 5

"As you can see, by purchasing a new $50,000 car every five years, our car buyer is incurring $1,195,617 in accounting costs over 50 years, and $3,577,190 in opportunity costs.

"Wow, that's a lot of money," said Gary.

"It really is," said Emily. "So, let's run it for $25,000 cars." She reworked the numbers and showed Gary the screen in Figure 6 on the opposite page. "By purchasing a late-model $25,000 used car every five years, our car buyer is incurring $597,809 in accounting costs over 50 years, and $1,788,595 in opportunity costs."

"Ouch. Still a lot."

"Yup," said Emily. "So, let's drop it down a little more, and see what purchasing a $15,000 car every five years will get you." (See Figure 7 on page 30.) "By purchasing an earlier-model $15,000 used car every five years, our car buyer is incurring $358,685 in accounting costs over 50 years, and $1,073,157 in opportunity costs."

"Oh," said Gary, looking disheartened. "Well, none of those numbers are encouraging. I mean, the last one more than the others, but still…. I don't understand, Emily, what am I supposed to do? I need to buy cars. I can't walk or hitchhike to work."

"No, of course you can't, Gary," Emily replied. "And no one is expecting you to. I run these charts for illustrative purposes, to show the financial impact of purchasing cars over a lifetime. I don't do any of it to suggest that you should *not* buy cars, or even the cars you like. It's only to encourage you to consider the *full economic costs* — the *accounting* and *opportunity costs* — of the cars you buy. Or any other major purchase, for that matter."

Gary thought for a moment, then turned to Emily looking dejected. "Well, now I'm thoroughly confused. I was pretty set on buying a new car with that $20,000."

Current Value of Assets:	10,000
Annual Savings:	10,000.00
Annual Savings Increase (%):	0.00%
Net ROR on Savings (%):	5.00%
Number of Years:	50
Year of 1st Purchase:	5

Auto Purchase Frequency	5
Actual Purchase Price:	25,000.00
Ann. Auto Price Increase (%):	3.00%
Sales Tax Rate (%):	0.00%
Ann. Auto Insurance	0.00
Ann. Insurance Increase (%):	

Title   Clear   NEW

Future Asset Val. WITHOUT Autos:	2,312,828
Cumulative Auto Costs:	(597,809)
Actual Asset Val. WITH Auto Costs:	524,233
True Cost Of Automobiles:	(1,788,595)

Yr	Annual Savings	EOY Asset Value NO Auto Costs	Automobile Purchase	Sales Tax	Cumulative Auto Costs	EOY Asset Value WITH Auto Costs	Loss of Future Asset Value
1	10,000	21,000				21,000	
2	10,000	32,550				32,550	
3	10,000	44,678				44,678	
4	10,000	57,411				57,411	
5	10,000	70,782	(28,138)		(28,138)	41,237	(29,545)
6	10,000	84,821			(28,138)	53,799	(31,022)
7	10,000	99,562			(28,138)	66,989	(32,573)
8	10,000	115,040			(28,138)	80,839	(34,202)
9	10,000	131,292			(28,138)	95,381	(35,912)
10	10,000	148,357	(32,619)		(60,757)	76,399	(71,958)
11	10,000	166,275			(60,757)	90,719	(75,555)
12	10,000	185,088			(60,757)	105,755	(79,333)
13	10,000	204,843			(60,757)	121,543	(83,300)
14	10,000	225,585			(60,757)	138,120	(87,465)
15	10,000	247,364	(37,815)		(98,572)	115,821	(131,544)
16	10,000	270,232			(98,572)	132,112	(138,121)
17	10,000	294,244			(98,572)	149,217	(145,027)
18	10,000	319,456			(98,572)	167,178	(152,278)
19	10,000	345,929			(98,572)	186,037	(159,892)
20	10,000	373,725	(43,838)		(142,409)	159,809	(213,916)
21	10,000	402,912			(142,409)	178,300	(224,612)
22	10,000	433,557			(142,409)	197,715	(235,843)
23	10,000	465,735			(142,409)	218,101	(247,635)

TruthConcepts.com

Figure 6

Automobile Purchase

Current Value of Assets:	10,000	
Annual Savings:	10,000.00	
Annual Savings Increase (%):	0.00%	
Net ROR on Savings (%):	5.00%	
Number of Years:	50	
Year of 1st Purchase:	5	

Auto Purchase Frequency	5
Actual Purchase Price:	15,000.00
Ann. Auto Price Increase (%):	3.00%
Sales Tax Rate (%):	0.00%
Ann. Auto Insurance	0.00
Ann. Insurance Increase (%):	

Title Clear NEW

Future Asset Val. WITHOUT Autos:	2,312,828
Cumulative Auto Costs:	(358,685)
Actual Asset Val. WITH Auto Costs:	1,239,671
True Cost Of Automobiles:	(1,073,157)

Yr	Annual Savings	EOY Asset Value NO Auto Costs	Automobile Purchase	Sales Tax	Cumulative Auto Costs	EOY Asset Value WITH Auto Costs	Loss of Future Asset Value
1	10,000	21,000				21,000	(17,727)
2	10,000	32,550				32,550	(18,613)
3	10,000	44,678				44,678	(19,544)
4	10,000	57,411				57,411	(20,521)
5	10,000	70,782	(16,883)		(16,883)	53,055	(21,547)
6	10,000	84,821			(16,883)	66,208	(43,175)
7	10,000	99,562			(16,883)	80,018	(45,333)
8	10,000	115,040			(16,883)	94,519	(47,600)
9	10,000	131,292			(16,883)	109,745	(49,980)
10	10,000	148,357	(19,572)		(36,454)	105,182	(52,479)
11	10,000	166,275			(36,454)	120,941	(78,926)
12	10,000	185,088			(36,454)	137,488	(82,872)
13	10,000	204,843			(36,454)	154,863	(87,016)
14	10,000	225,585			(36,454)	173,106	(91,367)
15	10,000	247,364	(22,689)		(59,143)	168,438	(95,935)
16	10,000	270,232			(59,143)	187,360	(128,350)
17	10,000	294,244			(59,143)	207,228	(134,767)
18	10,000	319,456			(59,143)	228,089	(141,506)
19	10,000	345,929			(59,143)	249,994	(148,581)
20	10,000	373,725	(26,303)		(85,446)	245,376	
21	10,000	402,912			(85,446)	268,145	
22	10,000	433,557			(85,446)	292,052	
23	10,000	465,735			(85,446)	317,154	

Figure 7

"And that may well be your decision, Gary. But let's talk about some other things first — let's talk about some things that could come up to bite you in the behind if you're not careful. What does your emergency fund look like, Gary, and your credit card debt?"

"Well, I owe about $2,000 on a credit card, and I just emptied my emergency fund again on a home repair for my mom—so, I'm back to zero on that."

"Mmmm. Well, here's some sad news, Gary. It's probably not something you want to hear, but it *is* the whole truth about your money. The bottom line is that you're running on a deficit. If you keep charging up your credit cards and zeroing out your emergency fund, your budget is not covering your expenses. You consistently run over."

"Um. Yes. I guess that's right."

"So, maybe this $20,000 is a great opportunity to begin reversing that tide, a chance for a new start. How about you zero-out that credit card and replenish that emergency fund? Replenish it with enough money to take the hits of an emergency when they come along."

"Okay. I guess that would be a good idea."

"And once you do that, I want you to take a friend out for a big piece of gourmet cheesecake, deliberately and specifically to celebrate the paying off of your credit card debt and the replenishing of your emergency fund."

"I like cheesecake."

"And here's the kicker, Gary. I want you to go ahead and buy that car. I want you to buy a great, late-model, reliable newer car — but perhaps just not a brand-spanking-new one, the kind that loses 30 percent of its value the moment you drive it off the lot."

"And the kind that triples my insurance bill each month."

"Exactly. Also, sell the one you're driving now. That may well put a few more thousand dollars into that car-buying budget."

"I can do that."

Emily handed Gary a small pamphlet. "And here's our Smart Car Buying guide. It's been written specifically for our clients, like you, to help navigate the car-buying landscape."

Gary took the pamphlet and looked down. "Thank you, Emily."

"You're welcome, Gary. It feels good to be free of debt. And having a healthy emergency fund as well will help you sleep at night — you, and the people who depend on you."

Gary sat silently and looked at the pamphlet.

"And you can *still* drive a newer car, Gary — just, like we said, not the brand-new kind." After a slight pause, Emily leaned back in her chair and drummed her fingers on the desk. "When you were at my presentation to your twelfth-grade class, do you remember what I said about interest and debt?"

"I do remember. I remember we're supposed to earn interest, not owe it—*Earn interest. Not owe it!*" Gary said with mock enthusiasm.

"Wow. Good job. I'm amazed you remember that. That was a long time ago."

"Well, I probably wouldn't be here if not for that great presentation you did. That really hit home."

"Thanks. And great. So, yeah, let's pay off that most likely high-interest credit card and replenish that emergency fund, so you don't need to run the card up again — then buy yourself that big piece of cheesecake and a lightly used car. Sound good?"

"Sounds good. Thanks, Emily."

"You got it. You're doing great. Keep up the good work!"

Smart Car Buying

In his book, *I Will Teach You To Be Rich*, Ramit Sethi encourages his readers to adhere to one principle: Spend lavishly on things that are important to you; cut ruthlessly on things that are not.

Now, discerning what actually *is* important to you—and what is not—can be no small task, especially with advertiser noise trying to interrupt that process at every turn.

Still, if brand new cars are just your thing, far be it from us to dissuade you. If new cars put the spring in your step, and the money is there, then have at it.

Still, whether you buy new, lightly used, or very used, a central tenet of the Prosperity Economics Movement is to make the most of every financial deal that comes your way. And that's exactly what this car-buying guide attempts to do. All in all, there are few bigger deals in life than buying a car, so let's see how we can make the most of that deal.

Car Talk

We were sad to receive the news of the passing of Tom Magliozzi while writing this book. He was one half of "Click and Clack," the nicknames he and his brother Ray went by on their beloved 25-year National Public Radio show, *Car Talk*.

Car Talk, and its companion website, CarTalk.com, provide some of the best car information out there, with expert reviews, rosters of highly-rated auto mechanics, and the secret tactics of car salesmen. The site also offers replays of the radio show. It is an invaluable resource for any car buyer, indeed any car owner.

One of the most important steps advanced by the brothers, whether buying new or used, is to review your prospective car's performance ratings as researched and reported by Consumer

Reports. The annual car-buying April issue of the print magazine can be found at most libraries—and a $30 ConsumerReports.org yearly membership not only supports this great consumer-advocacy group, it could save you thousands of dollars and untold disappointment and frustration with your car purchase.

If you're really feeling frugal, however, or only want the subscription for a short time, you can get it for just $6.95 monthly.

However you get the information, it's important to scour Consumer Reports' detailed road test reports, performance reviews, and the Best and Worst Values list. See how your prospective car choices measure up long before you enter a dealership.

For used-car purchases, the *Car Talk* guys emphasize again and again the absolute imperative step of getting a pre-purchase mechanical inspection. Especially essential when buying from a private party, this step is still extremely important even when buying from the most reputable high-end dealer, because even the dealers don't always know the exact condition of all the cars on their lots.

Once you've narrowed down to a particular year, make, and model, check out CarTalk.com's "Mechanic Files" for a highly rated mechanic in your area, and lay out the $100 to $150 for an in-depth pre-purchase inspection. It may be the best money you ever spend.

Once you've done your research, reviewed Consumer Reports, and gotten a pre-purchase inspection if you're buying used, it's time to start negotiating price.

One of the best resources we've found on this topic is the "Buying a Car" section on The Motley Fool website at Fool.com, started by brothers Tom and David Gardner. I don't necessarily endorse their stock-picking newsletters, but the website has some excellent resources. You'll find a comprehensive car buying section at Fool.com/car.

The author of the "Buying a Car" articles, Paul Maghielse, breaks down numerous steps to research, select, and purchase a car. When it comes to purchasing, however, one principle stands out as the golden rule in dealership price negotiation. This rule is comprised of three steps, which, Maghielse emphasizes, must be kept completely separate and followed in strict order. They are: negotiate price first, negotiate the value of your trade-in second, and arrange financing third.

Maghielse states that car salesmen will try to throw these issues all together, confounding buyers and obfuscating the bottom line. "These folk target customers like us for a living," he writes, "perhaps a dozen or more times a day, and they are remarkably skilled at controlling the direction of the deal.... Settling one matter at a time will prevent confusion—and confusion is a rather large weapon in their arsenal."

Salesmen may sit down, draw a four-square grid, and tell you about the great rebates, fantastic financing, and low monthly payments available if you buy today, all while sidestepping the key, most important issue at hand—the car's price.

Don't be fooled. Follow the three simple steps. Keep them distinctly separate and in strict order:

1. Negotiate price
2. Negotiate the value of your trade-in (if you have one)
3. Arrange financing

If the salesman continues to meld financing, price, and monthly payments, a simple response may be, "Hmmm. That's interesting. But right now I'm discussing *price only*." Repeat this phrase as often as you need to. If the salesman persists in entangling the issues, explain that you feel your wishes are not being respected and ask for a manager.

Great Financing?

The car dealership may in fact have a great financing deal; however, you will never know this unless you obtain your FICO credit score and shop around at your local banks and credit unions *first*. BankRate.com is an interest-rate-comparison site that also has great information. You need to do this *long before ever entering the dealer showroom*.

If your dealer can actually beat the bank or credit union's best auto loan rate, take it happily — but if they can't, stick with the other lender's deal. In either case, never ever discuss financing before negotiating the *price* of your car *first*.

Another important issue is that used-car loans often come at substantially higher interest rates than those for new cars. At 12 or 13 percent and higher, depending on your credit score, used-car loans can cost a bundle. The cash value portion of a whole life insurance policy not only provides a great savings vehicle, it can also offer a low 5–8 percent interest rate when borrowing against it, a great deal for financing a used car.

Car-Sales Trickery: Zero-Percent APR Versus Cash Rebate

Let's be aware that most car companies make as much, if not more, from *financing* their vehicles as they do from *manufacturing* them. Yet they often advertise interest rates as low as zero percent.

How is it that possible?

It's possible because car companies offer a different price *on the same car*, depending on your payment method.

If you get a quote of $30,000 on a car for cash, they may want to charge you $35,000 for that same car if you take the zero-percent financing.

So, you receive *either* a $5,000 rebate *or* a zero-percent financing deal. The dealer is incorporating a much higher interest rate into the *price* of the financed car—and then happily advertising zero percent to the public

This is why it's so important to compare rates from other lenders before walking into the dealership. And, once inside, to always *negotiate price first*.

Let's look at the numbers.

Assume you've taken the dealer up on her zero-percent financing deal. She quotes you a price of $35,000 financed for 48 months. If we look at Figure 8 below, we see what this monthly payment adds up to.

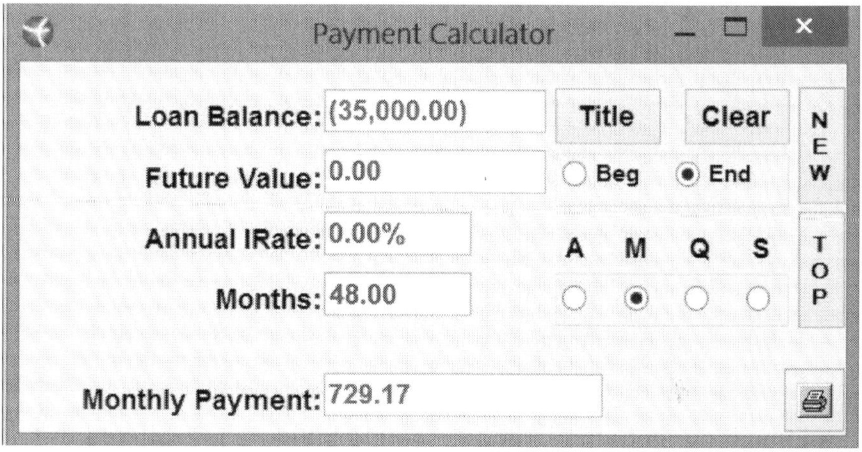

Figure 8

At zero percent, financing a $35,000 for 48 months results in a $729.17 monthly payment.

If your neighbor, however, goes to the *same* dealer to buy the *same* car and announces he will pay cash, the dealer may happily offer him a $5,000 rebate. Your neighbor has in fact gotten an auto loan from his local credit union, which will charge him 7.5 % due to his mediocre credit score. Figure 9 on the next page shows us the monthly payment on this deal.

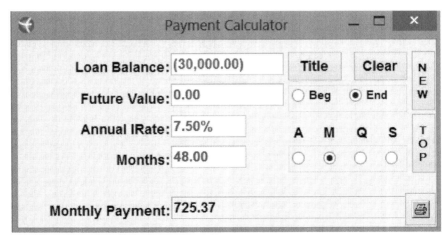

Figure 9

Financing $30,000 at 7.5 percent results in a monthly payment of $725.37 — actually *lower* than the $35,000 at zero percent—which amounts to a $729.17.

Adding $5000 to the *price* of the car equates to charging a 7.5 % interest without the price increase. The $5,000 is in fact the interest of a 7.5 % new car loan — a very high interest rate for a new auto loan at today's writing — added up-front to the price of the car.

The same tactic is used for 1.9 percent and other abnormally low interest rates advertised by car dealers. And know that their cash rebate policies are not always advertised.

What is important to remember is that the *amount financed* — the total price of the car —always has a larger impact on the monthly payment than any nominal change in interest rate.

That is why we always negotiate *price first*.

The real money is saved or squandered negotiating the *price* of the car, not the interest on the auto loan financing. Don't confuse the two. And don't let your salesperson either.

Fax-A-Thon

The last tactic we'd like to briefly touch on, and the one we advocate, is an unconventional method of *new-car* price negotiation called the fax-a-thon method — having undoubtedly evolved into the email-a-thon method in recent years.

Paul Maghielse, in his "Buying a Car" series on Fool.com/Car, emphasizes that new cars are commodities, rolling off the assembly line every few minutes. New-car prices, their rebates, price shifts, and incentives change with market forces, sometimes on a daily basis.

People often take note of where to find a cheaper gallon of milk or loaf of bread, but won't take advantage of market forces when buying a new car, instead heading off to the closest dealership to have an audience with whatever master salesperson is on the showroom floor.

The Motley Fool offers the fax/email-a-thon method of new-car buying instead.

To recount this strategy, in a nutshell, a car buyer will research and build her new car online, using reviews and ratings from Consumer Reports, CarTalk.com, and any other reliable sources. Once settled, from her online research, on the make, model, and options of her car choice, and a visit to a nearby dealership that results in a test drive *only*, she will obtain the fax number or email addresses of the fleet managers of every dealership— of her make and model— within 100 miles.

With a detailed options specifications list and personalized cover letter, the car buyer will fax or email each and every fleet manager to say she will be taking pricing bids for her particular model within the next three days. The dealer with the lowest bid gets her sale. The managers typically return faxes or emails with their bids. Lowest bid wins. Sometimes, there are several rounds.

The fax/email-a-thon method requires no dealership visit, no confusing price with monthly payments, and no salesman theater — just the best price for a new car.

It is worthy to note that we conducted a preliminary survey of new-car pricing guides by Kelly Blue Book, Edmunds, and True Car. These guides offered new-car pricing they called "Fair price," "Average Price," and "True Price." Between these three sources, we received prices that varied by $8,000 for the exact same make, model, and optioned car —an astronomical price range that demonstrated that new-car prices are indeed a flexible and moving target.

So, be sure to do extensive online research, narrow down your choices, make a test-drive *only* visit to the dealership, and drive a hard bargain when negotiating for a car, whether sitting across from a used-car dealer or fielding fax or email bids from a new one.

Remember never to confuse price with monthly payments, and always negotiate price first before even introducing trade-in values or car loans into the discussion. And don't let yourself get ambushed with a high-pressure warranty sales pitch, especially if you have the savings to handle car repairs as they come. (See sidebar next page.)

And lastly, refer back to the Truth Concepts Auto Purchasing calculators at the beginning of this section. Remember that car buying is one of the biggest expenses you'll incur in your lifetime, so calculate both accounting and opportunity costs for all your car-buying decisions and be sure the whole truth about your money is in the driver's seat.

A Warning About Warranties

There's one final challenge you'll likely encounter when purchasing a car. If you're buying from a dealer, they are going to try to sell you a service warranty that can add 20 percent or more to the payments you'll make... even if the car is still under another warranty! They may also try to sell you extra insurance to cover the loan amount should something happen to the car.

Most purchasers don't get their money's worth out of their car warranties. And this is another reason why saving money is key. If you have savings, you won't need a warranty unless you insist on driving a car known to be prone to a lot of issues, which I'd recommend against.

If you decide you do want a warranty, realize that it is also negotiable. You don't have to pay full price for it. You don't have to finance it. You don't have to buy that particular warranty from them right that minute. Do your homework and get the best warranty at the best price, not the one forced on you as you're signing papers."

Take your time, do your research, and don't buy something you're not sure you want under pressure.

CHAPTER 3

Mortgages: Weighing Your Finance Options

Several years passed and Gary continued to do well at his job. His first meeting with Emily Peterson had paid off, and Gary kept his credit cards low and his emergency fund high —and his slightly used car was still looking good and going strong.

But life reared its head, as Emily said it would. Gary's mother and sister had needs their modest incomes couldn't always cover. There were medical bills and car repairs and the house Gary grew up in certainly wasn't new. It always needed a pipe fixed or an appliance replaced, and that hit everyone's budget hard.

By now Gary was renting a nice but small $500 per month apartment near his family. Try as he may to save up for a down payment to buy a house, something with more urgency and greater priority always took place.

But then the greatest and most urgent priority that Gary had known so far came to pass. Gary's aunt, the woman who helped raise him and who'd always treated him like her own son, became ill.

Gary's mother was devastated. She spent every spare waking moment with her sister, driving her to the hospital and various treatments, but Gary's mom had to work as well. Gary joined his mother and his own sister in caring for his aunt, but things had not slowed down at work. Gary had become a full-fledged superintendent, and he now ran entire construction projects on his own. Work days were long and tiring, and there was little time for days off.

In fact, despite Gary using every last bit of his paid leave during his aunt's illness in a matter of months, he was still left wondering why, at the end of a person's life, they couldn't have their family relaxed, present, attentive, and available around them — instead of haggard, frazzled, and distracted. It all seemed for nothing, he thought, if you couldn't be there for the people you loved when it counted most.

When Gary's aunt succumbed to her illness, he took two weeks of unpaid leave to be there for his very shaken mother, his sister, and to wrap his own head around this new normal. They were a small family, but they were close. And now, they were one fewer.

A couple weeks later, Gary's mother was cleaning out her sister's things and came across a document. It was a life insurance policy. The beneficiary listed on the policy was her own son. Unbeknownst to anyone, Gary's aunt had kept up with the policy her entire life. Gary was the beneficiary of a $100,000 benefit.

As Gary and his mom stood in the kitchen looking at the check, they both had an eerie sense of déjà vu.

"Well, it seems as though we've been here before, son, though under better circumstances." Gary's mother wiped her eyes. "This is an even bigger check than the last time we stood here." She laughed through recently shed tears.

"Yeah," said Gary. "And I still don't know what to do with it." Gary's heart ached for his mother and his beloved aunt, but he was still serious about his statement.

They both stood quiet for a while, feeling the strange irony of it all.

Then, after a long silence, Gary's mom said, "Your house, honey. Your house. This is money for your house. You've taken care of ours for so long. Now it's time for you to have your own." Then after a long pause, she went on, "Your aunt would have wanted it. Your aunt would have wanted it."

It was true. His aunt would have wanted it. She even spoke of it. She would cut out little listings in the paper and give them to him, she was a open-house addict and stopped at every one she passed. She was on the lists of 12 realtors. In many ways, it was plainly obvious.

"Before you do, though," his mom went on, "why don't you see that woman again, that financial advisor. She seemed to do well by you last time. This would seem another good time to pay her a visit."

"I will, Mom. I will." Gary put his hand on his mom's shoulder. They looked at each other and all that passed in the last 30-odd years flashed before them.

* * * * * * * *

"I'm so sorry to hear about your aunt, Gary." Emily Peterson spoke quietly as she sat across the large wooden desk from him.

"Thank you, Emily. She was a really sweet person. I was lucky to have known her for all this time."

"I have no doubt. And you had no idea about the life insurance policy?"

"None at all. Not until my mother found the papers. I wonder why she never said anything."

"Wow. That's a mystery. It's quite a bit of money. The last

time you were here we were only talking about a fraction of that amount."

"This is true. Yes, $100,000 is much more. But, Emily, I think I know what I want to do with it. I want to buy a house. I want to buy it outright, to pay cash."

"Wow, Gary. Congratulations. That's exciting news. And paying cash is a gutsy move; it's the right move for many people. Still, I'm a Prosperity Economics Advisor and my mission is to tell the whole truth about your money. So would it be OK if I showed you a few things?"

"Yes, Emily," Gary answered, "of course. That's why I'm here."

"All righty. Good. So, just so you know, home ownership is a different creature than renting. No landlord will pay for repairs or for ongoing maintenance to your place. On account of this, money needs to be set aside for those things…because that water heater *will* go out and the refrigerator *will* need to be replaced."

"Oh, you don't have to tell me. I've been dealing with my mother's house for years."

"OK. Well, then you also know there are taxes due every year on your property, and home owner's insurance."

"Yes, I do. I know that very well — all of that on top of the mortgage payment.

"And that's why I want to pay cash," Gary went on, "then I don't have to think about at least *that* monthly payment. Plus, paying for the house in cash will save me tens of thousands of dollars in interest, won't it?"

"It may save you an interest payment, but it won't save you an interest *cost*," replied Emily. "In fact, let's go to the calculators right now."

Emily opened her Truth Concepts software and brought up a

Loan Analysis calculator. "Let's see how much interest you'd save by paying cash versus, let's say, taking out a 15-year mortgage."

Emily entered the inputs for the loan's terms:

- $100,000 loan balance
- fifteen-year (180 months) term
- 5% interest rate.

Emily turned her computer screen towards Gary and showed him the calculator in Figure 10 (next page).

"As you can see, taking no mortgage would save you $42,343 in interest versus taking out a 15-year mortgage."

Wow, thought Gary, *$42,343 — that's a lot of money.* He was dumb-founded, but he was also impressed with his financial savvy for deciding to buy his house outright.

"In fact, while we're at it," said Emily, "let's run the numbers for a 30-year mortgage."

Gary leaned in as Emily changed the loan timeframe in the Loan Analysis calculator:

- $100,000 loan balance
- thirty-year (360 months) term
- 5% interest rate

Up popped the table in Figure 11 (next page spread).

Gary was aghast.

"I'm not sure I even believe this," said Gary. "I would pay $93,256 in interest for taking out a $100,000 mortgage over 30 years? That's almost double the cost of the house!"

"Yup," said Emily. "That's what the bank charges you for bor-rowing their $100,000. It's the mechanics of compound interest. It's important to understand those mechanics before you purchase any big-ticket item — and the biggest item most anyone will purchase in their lifetime is a house.

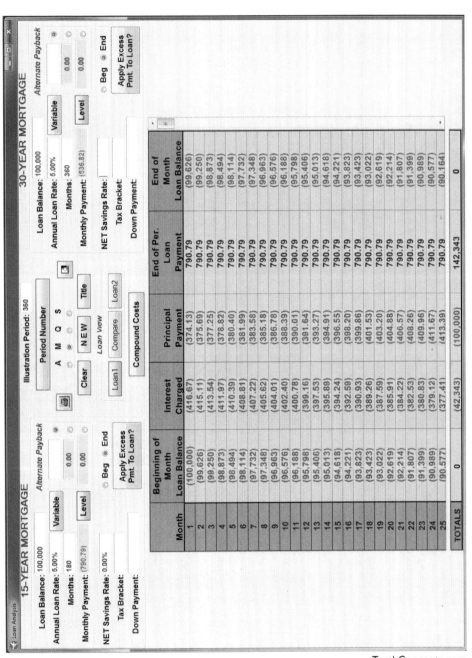

Figure 10

TruthConcepts.com

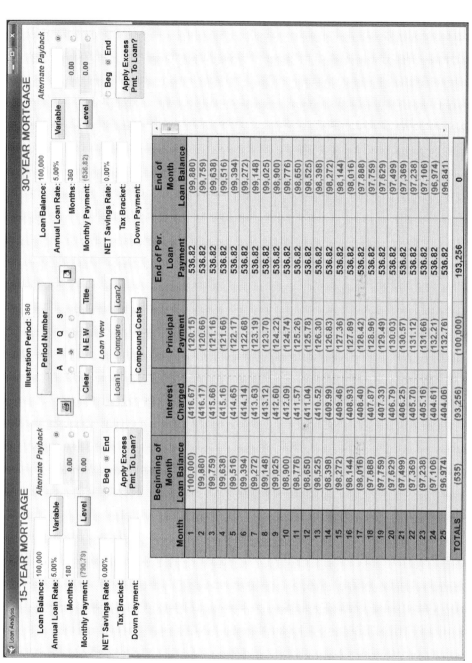

TruthConcepts.com

Figure 11

"You'll pay almost double for that house, Gary—close to $200,000— if you take out a loan for 30 years."

Wow, thought Gary again. He couldn't quite believe his ears. $93,256.00 for the privilege of purchasing a home over time? *No way,* he thought, feeling a little bit nauseated. *No way am I paying the bank that kind of money. Thank God, but mostly thank Aunt Emma, for the $100,000 to put down in cash.*

"Well, that settles it," he said. "I'm buying my house for cash. Thank you so much, Emily, for clarifying my options and running those scenarios for me. I'm so glad I came in to see you."

"I'm glad you came in to see me too, Gary. It was really nice seeing you again. But, just before you go, would you mind if I run another calculation or two for you?"

"Um, OK," said Gary. *I'm not sure what more there is to be said,* he thought, *but OK.*

"The trick with comparing mortgages," she started, "is to look at the value of the money over time. While it appears that a 15-year mortgage costs less than a 30-year mortgage from the calculations we just did, and cash appears to cost the least, the reality is that you only pay less *in interest.*"

"But besides the principal," Gary interjected, "which was $100,000 in both mortgages we looked at, what else is there to pay besides interest?"

"Opportunity cost," Emily answered. "In other words, by putting your money into a mortgage, what *opportunity* are you giving up elsewhere? Now, true opportunity cost, in classic economics, looks at *the next-best potential use of the money or resource.* However, that could be many things—you could put your $100,000 into buying ten cars or collectible art or starting a company or the stock market. It's somewhat subjective. But more importantly, it's impractical to compare every possible use of your money to try to determine what's the 'next-best use.' You follow me?"

"Definitely."

"Okay. So, for our purposes, which is primarily to illustrate the value of the money itself over time—apart from what you could use it for—it makes the most sense to see what that money could grow to if put into a fairly predictable and safe place. Then, we can truly compare dollars to dollars and determine what your mortgage options actually cost you when taking into account *the loss of use of that money.*"

She looked at Gary to make sure he was still on track, and he nodded. Emily turned her computer monitor a little more towards Gary so it was easier for him to see.

"This is a Future Value calculator," she said. "It's simply a compound-interest calculator, which calculates the interest earned on money placed in an interest-bearing account. In other words, it'll show you the *future value* of your money. Does that make sense?"

"Yep."

"Good. Do you remember, back in the day, when I talked to your high school class about the mechanics of compound interest?"

"I remember that we should earn interest, not owe it." Gary sing-songed the last five words.

"Yes, that's right. Wow, so I guess that stuck, huh? Good! So, when you take out a mortgage, those mechanics are working in the bank's favor. But when you deposit money in an interest-bearing account, it's like *you* are loaning the bank *your* money. And you get paid for that. Get it?"

"I do."

"Perfect. So let's take a look at the $100,000 your aunt left you, and let's say you put it into an interest-bearing account paying 5 percent. This could be any type of bank account, a certificate of deposit, money market, or cash value life insurance. With me so far?"

"Yes, I am."

"Okay. So, let's see what that adds up to."

Emily entered the inputs and pointed to the table in Figure 12.

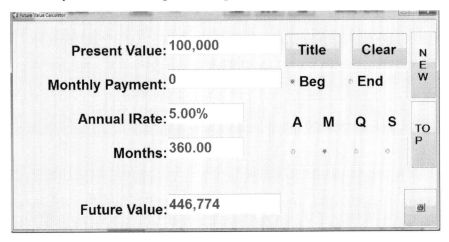

Figure 12

The number in the bottom Future Value field was $446,774.

"Gary, $100,000 invested at 5 percent over 30 years grows to $446,774—over four times what you put into it."

"Wow!" Gary said. "$446,774... seriously?"

"Yep," Emily answered. "Nearly half a million dollars. And this is what we're assigning as the opportunity cost associated with your getting a mortgage—what you *could have* earned with that hundred grand if you did *not* put it into a house."

"That almost makes me want to live in a van instead of buying a house."

"Well, Gary, I'm gonna go out on a limb and say you probably wouldn't want to for 30 years."

"Good point."

"But here's the thing," Emily continued. "We want to compare this with your mortgage costs because, remember, we're trying to see which mortgage—or no mortgage by paying all cash—costs the least. So, to do this, we go back to the Loan Analysis calculator. But this go-around, we factor in the 5 percent Net Savings Rate that we didn't before. We're going to take into consideration that the money going into this mortgage is *not* being put into 5-percent interest-bearing savings."

"Because every payment going toward the mortgage is money I could have put into earning interest?"

"Exactly," she said. "You are denying yourself the opportunity—this is, again, opportunity cost—the ability to earn interest on that money."

"Okay. Got it. And my mortgage interest paid and savings interest earned, the two rates, those are set at 5 percent so we have an equal comparison... is that right?"

"Yes. Good catch. With any financial comparison, you must only change one variable at a time; otherwise, you're comparing apples to oranges. We're looking at the cost of your mortgages, 15 versus 30 years, so every other factor needs to be the same."

"All right," Gary said with a nod. "Let's see how this looks."

Emily pulled up the result, shown in Figure 13 (next page). "There you go. Believe it or not, both the 15-year and 30-year mortgages have the same exact compound cost—$446,774. 'Compound cost' is just the term we use for factoring in the time value of the money."

"And," Gary said, "when we came up with the same number in the Future Value Calculator, how does that tie in?"

"That would still be, in a sense, your compound cost if you paid $100,000 cash for the house. Think of that scenario as loaning your-

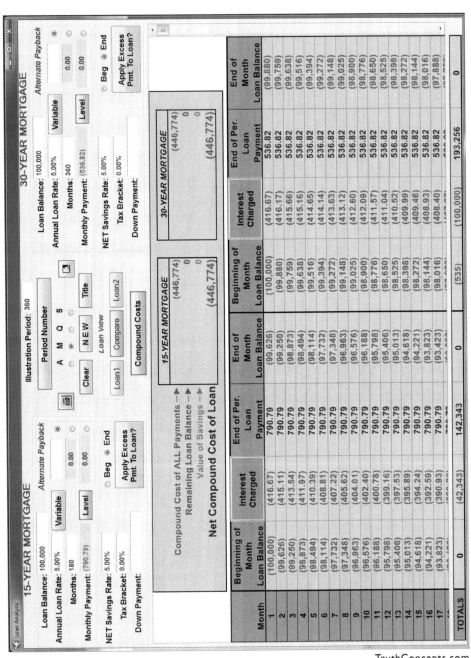

TruthConcepts.com

Figure 13

self the money, like you are both the mortgage company and the borrower. You loaned yourself the $100,000 by effectively taking it away from being put into your own savings, and thus you 'paid' 5 percent in annual interest because it was 5 percent you could not earn on the money each year."

"Oh, I see. Wow… so whether I pay cash, take a 15-year mortgage, or take a 30-year mortgage, the use of that money is costing me the same over time."

"Yep. Again, you'll pay less *in interest* on the 15-year mortgage, but overall—when factoring in the time value of money—all three financing scenarios end up costing the same."

"Okay. But then, with everything being equal, why not just pay cash, and then I don't have any mortgage payment to worry about?"

"There's no doubt that most people would feel a huge peace of mind in having no mortgage payment. And peace of mind is worth something. But my job is to show you the economics of your choices. You'll have to ultimately decide on the emotional aspect, your comfort level, but it's important to at least first understand the totality of the situation so you can make the best choice for you. When you have all the information, you can feel assured that you've made your decision with complete understanding."

Gary nodded, and Emily reached into a tray on her desk and pulled out a sheet of paper.

"Gary, being a Prosperity Economics Advisor, I'm guided by seven Principles of Prosperity. Read out loud the fifth principle for me." Emily handed him the Principles of Prosperity handout shown on the next page.

SUMMARY OF THE
7 PRINCIPLES OF PROSPERITY™

1. THINK — Owning a Prosperity mindset eliminates Poverty; scarcity thinking keeps you stuck.

2. SEE — Increase your Prosperity by adopting a macro-economic point of view—a perspective in which you can see how each one of your economic decisions affects all the others. Avoid micro-economic "tunnel vision."

3. MEASURE — Awareness and measurement of opportunity costs enables you to recover them. Ignore this at your peril.

4. FLOW — The true measure of Prosperity is cashflow. Don't focus on net worth alone.

5. CONTROL — Those with the gold make the rules; stay in control of your money rather than relinquishing control to others.

6. MOVE — The velocity of money is the movement of dollars through assets. Movement accelerates Prosperity; accumulation slows it down. Avoid accumulation.

7. MULTIPLY — Prosperity comes readily when your money "multiplies"—meaning that one dollar does many jobs. Your money is disabled when each dollar performs only one or two jobs.

Gary read:

Control

*Those with the gold make the rules; stay in control of
your money rather than relinquishing control to others.*

"Yes," Emily said. "Maintaining control and decision-making power over your money is a key principle. When you hand $100,000 in cash over to buy a property, your control over that money disappears."

Emily paused for a moment, then became very serious.

"But there's something far more important, Gary," she said quietly.

"Remember telling me how much you wished you could be there for your aunt as she became ill? Remember telling me how much you cared for her, how she helped raise you as a child and had been there for you your entire life, through thick and thin?"

Gary nodded and dropped his eyes to the floor.

"Remember telling me how sick it made you to watch her suffer, knowing you couldn't walk away from your job and regular paycheck, and that you'd used up all your time off?"

Gary choked back some emotion. He was silent.

Emily continued on quietly, "Well, imagine if at that time you'd had some money to fall back on. Imagine if there had been money in the bank to simply say to your boss, 'My aunt is ill. She helped raise me, and she needs me now. I'm going to be there for her.'

"You could have also said, 'I hope my job is here when I return. But if not, then that's okay. My family is my priority now. And I'm not going to confuse my priorities."

Gary remained silent and still. He could not meet Emily's eyes.

"I'm not saying this to drive a stake into your wounds, Gary.

I'm saying it because, regardless of the amount that money grows to in 30 years, having a cash reserve at every stage in life is imperative — cash that is available, accessible, and ready to use when life hits you, broadside, just as it did you and your aunt this past year."

Gary finally looked up.

"And though I don't want to be morose, Gary, life can be completely upended in a minute."

Gary looked wide-eyed.

"But it's not only the most drastic of circumstances we're considering here. Let's work with something not so dire. What if the roof on that house of yours needs replacing in 15 years? Or the water heater? Or you told me you're planning on getting married soon. What if you could pay for that wedding in cash?"

Emily watched Gary thoughtfully.

"Imagine being debt free after the wedding? Or after making improvements on your property? Having the cash around to address those situations can be the difference between serious stress and overwhelm and a feeling of peace and calm.

"You're still young, Gary. Get some miles on you and you'll realize having a cash reserve can be pivotal, in the good times and the bad, throughout every stage in your life."

Gary listened quietly.

"So," Emily continued, "just for argument's sake, let's say you couldn't keep your savings untouched for 30 years, and you needed to tap that money in half the time. Let's see what that $100,000 would grow to if you stuck it in an account for 15 years."

Emily entered some inputs and brought up the Future Value chart in Figure 14.

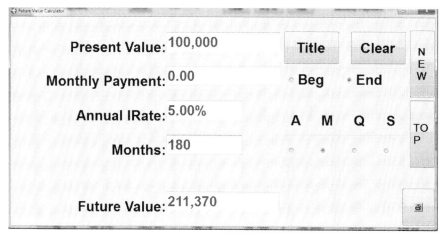

Figure 14

"After 15 years, you'd have $211,370.

"How much time could that buy you, Gary, if you had to go through it all again with your mother, your sister, or a friend?"

"A lot of time," Gary replied, "$211,370 would buy me a lot of time," and then more lightly, "and in the best-case scenario, a lot of new roofs and water heaters."

Emily smiled, "Yes. A lot of new roofs and water heaters."

Gary sat quietly for a while, considering his potential cash reserve. Then, Emily's thoughts seemed to shift.

"One more thing, Gary. Know this. Success is discipline. These methods, the methods of Prosperity Economics, are not for the faint of heart. They're not for everyone."

"Oh?" replied Gary.

"No. Having an accessible and available $100,000 laying around, compounding into even more money every year, can be tempting—tempting enough to blow on exotic vacations or a man cave in your new home."

"True."

"So, if you feel you're the type of person who will access that money indiscriminately or without regard, then this strategy is not for you. In that case, you should absolutely buy your house for cash. You can always take what *would have* been your mortgage payment and stick it into an interest-bearing account each month. In fact, if you do that and earn 5 percent each year, you'll wind up with the same $211,370 after 15 years and $446,774 after 30 years—if you can maintain the resolve not to touch it."

"Ummm."

"And there's no judgment in that, at all, Gary. Knowing yourself is a wise and responsible way to go through life. Alternately, making minimum credit card payments or trying to impress friends with your dear aunt's bequest is not."

"Well, that's definitely not me."

"I'm confident of that, Gary. You know I'm mostly making a point. Keeping the money in your control, following that Principle of Prosperity Economics, puts that money there to catch you when you fall—or someone you love. It's for that or for helping you reach financial independence. Either one. But it's not to tap into when you are tempted to overspend one month or to make up for the habit of overspending."

Gary listened soberly. Emily's tone was serious and a bit severe, but it didn't throw him. Gary had known people who had received generous gifts, large bonus checks, and other substantial lump sums and blown them in a year, ending up with nothing to show. He wasn't fazed by Emily's sternness.

They sat in silence for a moment. Then Gary whispered, "Big hat. No cattle."

"What...?" said Emily.

Gary chimed again, "Big hat. No cattle. My grandfather used to say it. It refers to people who prance around in fancy things but ultimately don't have a pot to… well, you know… don't have a chamber pot."

"Yes, I do know," laughed Emily. "I'm a financial advisor. I do know. It's important to own a chamber pot, Gary, long before you own fancy things. It's important to have ground under your feet, a roof over your head, and a savings to fall back on—and to make that your first priority."

"Mmmm."

"But that's not to say you shouldn't enjoy your windfall, Gary. Take 10 percent right now and go out and spend it on something you love. Maybe go on a fancy honeymoon after the wedding, or furnish that house of yours. It's not all gloom and doom. You should be able to enjoy some of your money at the time you receive it."

"That would be great, Emily. I would really like that."

"Excellent."

"Wow," he said. "I really got more than I bargained for on this visit! I wasn't counting on all this information and the new perspective."

"Good, Gary. That new perspective is what I'm counting on, so I'm glad you came to it. It's why I do this. But you're not getting off that easy. I've got one more calculation to show you."

"What?"

"Yes. Let's run through one more scenario."

"Okay, okay, fine." He smiled at his feigned exasperation.

"With all the talk of compounding interest, we haven't talked about the mortgage interest tax deduction the government hands out as an incentive for taking out a mortgage."

"What?"

"Yep, it's true. So let's do that."

Emily pulled up the Loan Analysis calculator they'd been

working on and entered the inputs for a $100,000 loan at 5% over 30 years. Gary saw that Emily entered values into two fields that until now had remained blank: the Tax Bracket field and the NET Savings Rate field. She pointed to the chart in Figure 15A.

"OK, Gary. In column four, titled End of Period Loan Payment, we see the monthly payment of your 30-year mortgage — $536.82."

"Yep, I see that," said Gary.

"Good. Now to the left of that, the second column, titled Interest Charged, is the proportion of that monthly payment going to interest every month.

"Even though your payment stays the same each month at $536.82, the proportion of it going to interest decreases just a little every month as the proportion of it going to principal increases by the same amount. With me so far?"

"Yes," Gary replied.

"Excellent. The reason for this, as column one labeled Beginning of Month Loan Balance shows you, is that your total loan balance, the entirety of the mortgage, decreases each month with every mortgage payment."

"Oh, I see." answered Gary.

"Yes. Not so hard, huh? Now, let's look at something new. This is different.

"The far-right column, titled Value of Savings @ 5%, is a new calculation.

"The reasoning behind it goes like this: Because the government wants to encourage home ownership, and because they know most people cannot afford to pay cash to buy their homes outright, the government allows you to deduct your mortgage interest from your taxes.

"That means that the interest you pay on your mortgage each

30-YEAR MORTGAGE

Loan Balance: 100,000
Annual Loan Rate: 5.00% [Variable]
Months: 360
Monthly Payment: (536.82) [Level]
NET Savings Rate: 5.00%
Tax Bracket: 25.00%
Down Payment: 0

Alternate Payback
0.00
0.00
○ Beg ● End
Apply Excess Pmt To Loan?

Illustration Period: 360
Period Number
A M Q S
Clear   N E W   Title
Loan View
Loan1   Compare   Loan2
Compound Costs

Loan Balance: 0
Annual Loan Rate: 0.00%   Months: 0
Monthly Payment: 0.00
NET Savings Rate: 0.00%
Tax Bracket: 0.00%
Down Payment:

Alternate Payback
0.00
0.00
○ Beg ● End
Apply Excess Pmt To Loan?

Month	Beginning of Month Loan Balance	Interest Charged	Principal Payment	End of Per. Loan Payment	End of Month Loan Balance	Interest Deduction Tax Savings	Value Of Tax Savings @ 5.00%
1	(100,000)	(416.67)	(120.15)	536.82	(99,880)	104	104
2	(99,880)	(416.17)	(120.66)	536.82	(99,759)	104	209
3	(99,759)	(415.66)	(121.16)	536.82	(99,638)	104	313
4	(99,638)	(415.16)	(121.66)	536.82	(99,516)	104	419
5	(99,516)	(414.65)	(122.17)	536.82	(99,394)	104	524
6	(99,394)	(414.14)	(122.68)	536.82	(99,272)	104	630
7	(99,272)	(413.63)	(123.19)	536.82	(99,148)	103	736
8	(99,148)	(413.12)	(123.70)	536.82	(99,025)	103	842
9	(99,025)	(412.60)	(124.22)	536.82	(98,900)	103	949
10	(98,900)	(412.09)	(124.74)	536.82	(98,776)	103	1,056
11	(98,776)	(411.57)	(125.26)	536.82	(98,650)	103	1,163
12	(98,650)	(411.04)	(125.78)	536.82	(98,525)	103	1,271
13	(98,525)	(410.52)	(126.30)	536.82	(98,398)	103	1,378
14	(98,398)	(409.99)	(126.83)	536.82	(98,272)	102	1,487
15	(98,272)	(409.46)	(127.36)	536.82	(98,144)	102	1,595
16	(98,144)	(408.93)	(127.89)	536.82	(98,016)	102	1,704
17	(98,016)	(408.40)	(128.42)	536.82	(97,888)	102	1,813
18	(97,888)	(407.87)	(128.96)	536.82	(97,759)	102	1,923
19	(97,759)	(407.33)	(129.49)	536.82	(97,629)	102	2,033
20	(97,629)	(406.79)	(130.03)	536.82	(97,499)	102	2,143
21	(97,499)	(406.25)	(130.57)	536.82	(97,369)	102	2,253
22	(97,369)	(405.70)	(131.12)	536.82	(97,238)	101	2,364
23	(97,238)	(405.16)	(131.66)	536.82	(97,106)	101	2,475
24	(97,106)	(404.61)	(132.21)	536.82	(96,974)	101	2,587
25	(96,974)	(404.06)	(132.76)	536.82	(96,841)	101	2,699
TOTALS	(535)	(93,256)	(100,000)	193,256	(0)	23,314	0

TruthConcepts.com

Figure 15A

year can be subtracted from your taxable income — whatever it amounts to won't be taxed."

"Um, OK," replied Gary, looking confused and unimpressed.

"So. Let's put it this way. You're in the 25% tax bracket, correct? After all your exemptions and deductions are tallied, the top level of your income will be taxed at 25%."

"Yes, that's correct," replied Gary.

"So that last column is just that. It's 25% of the mortgage interest displayed in column two. The first value in the far-right column is $104. That's 25% of the first value in the second column, $416.67. For your income level, this is what you would save in taxes for that month."

"OK. I see that," responded Gary.

"Excellent. So this is where it gets a bit confusing. The far-right column is not just a straight 25% of the interest shown in column two—it is the cumulative sum of that interest each month, increasing by a factor of 5%."

"Um," muttered Gary.

"For instance, let's take month number seven. The interest due that month is $413.63, and 25% of that equals $103. Added to the value of the previous month six, $630, that only equals $733. The reason month seven is three dollars more, $736, is because of the 5% interest that's been compounding since the beginning."

"Oh, okay, I get it," said Gary.

"Yeah. So there are a couple calculations going on over there. Keep that in mind."

"Okay," said Gary.

"So, Gary, take a look at month 12, in the Value of Savings column. What is the amount there?"

"$1,271."

"Correct. Excellent. That's your tax savings that first year."

Gary looked confused and then asked, "So this all means I'll have to calculate my anticipated mortgage interest tax deduction, pull it out of my salary, and invest it every month?"

"Well, no," answered Emily, "the deduction happens automatically when you file your taxes—you report the interest you pay, which causes the deduction, *and* your income on the same tax form. If you'd paid cash, you wouldn't get the deduction. So treat the deduction as a bonus. Save it and leave your emergency account alone."

"OK. Well, how much money could I earn?"

"As we saw, $1,271 for the first year, to start. But let's extrapolate that out to the end of the loan, to month 360 at the bottom of that far-right column. Do you know what you would have?"

"Nope."

"After investing your mortgage interest tax savings for 30 years at 5%, you'd have $63,580." She showed him the screen in Figure 15B on the next page.

Gary was again silent. He couldn't believe all this money could result from simply putting his inheritance into a savings, investment, or cash value life insurance account — and pulling his mortgage payment from his paycheck.

"And by the way," Emily continued, "what I just showed you is another reason why 15-year mortgages are not better than 30-year ones. Because you pay less in interest on a 15-year mortgage, that means you also get less of a tax deduction. So, when you factor in the time value of saving that tax deduction on a 15-year mortgage, you actually come out worse off than doing the same with a 30-year mortgage. You also won't have that $63,580 tax benefit if you pay cash for the house, either!" (See Figure 16, next page spread.)

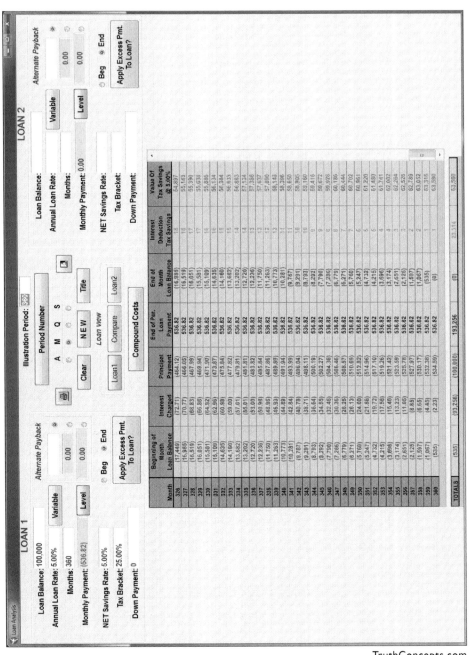

TruthConcepts.com

Figure 15B

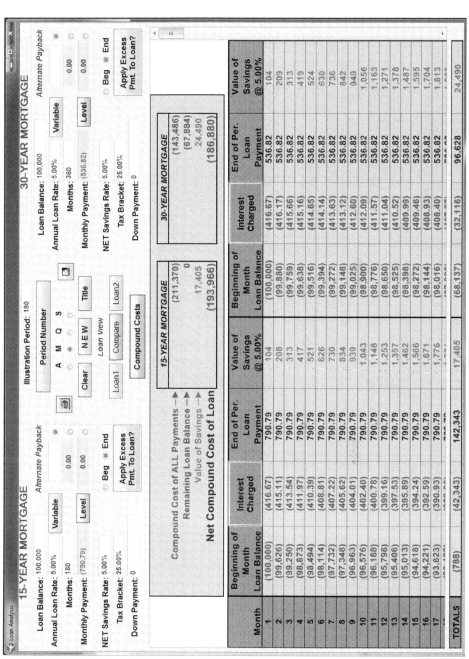

TruthConcepts.com

Figure 16

"Interesting," Gary said. "That makes sense."

"Now remember, all of this will require you to make that mortgage payment from your salary, and not simply let that money flow into your general expenses, as would likely be your choice if you paid cash. I hope you understand the point, now that you have seen what kind of return it would get you."

Gary nodded.

"Most importantly, though, as your aunt's inheritance grows over your lifetime, you will have access to it. It's money that is there in case you lose your job, if another family member becomes sick, or that house of yours needs major repair. It's there for you to fall back on. Remember, that's the 'Control' aspect we talked about earlier."

Gary remained silent. After a moment, he asked:

"But all my friends say I should put down as much as I can on the house. They're all saving up diligently for their own down payments, trying to save as much as they can before taking out a mortgage."

"Great that they're saving, but not great that they'll put that money into the house. Remember how we saw that the cost of the house over time is the same whether you pay cash, take out a 15-year mortgage, or take out a 30-year mortgage? Well, the same thing applies whether you pay all cash or part in cash—in other words, a down payment. So, this brings us back again to control of your money. Whatever you put down, whether it's 10 percent or 20 percent or whatever, you've lost control of that money."

"But it's equity, right? I mean, I can take out a home-equity loan if I needed to, right?"

"True. But the thing is, you have to apply for it and qualify for it, it goes on your credit, and worst of all, you end up paying interest to the bank to use that money! Actually, the worst of it is that your house is on the line—if something bad happens and you default on that home-equity loan, you could lose your home."

Gary let that sink in before Emily continued.

"Conversely, if you keep the money out of the house and in a savings-type account, you have two options. One, you can access it at no cost by withdrawing from your savings account, although you would incur opportunity cost since you removed principal and have now lost the ability to earn interest on that money. Or two, you can borrow against it with far less risk. In cash value life insurance, for example, if you couldn't pay that loan back—ever, in your entire life—nothing would happen to your credit, you wouldn't lose your home, and the repayment would just come out of your death benefit."

"Wow," he said. "So, minimum down is really the way to go?"

"Yep," she said. "Keep control of your money. Everything you put into the house is at risk until you own it outright. You could make 300 payments perfectly on time, 25 years into your mortgage, and if something happens that causes you to default on your payments, you could lose all that money you paid *and* your house. Conversely, your money kept outside of the house, building up in a reliable interest-bearing account, that's your safety net in the event anything happens."

"All right, Emily. You've sold me. Minimum down on the house, and I'll save and invest my aunt's money."

"Perfect. You have an amazing opportunity here. You have the chance to buy the house *and* maintain a growing cash reserve over your lifetime. Many people don't have this opportunity—and many, if they have it, don't take advantage of it."

Gary nodded in complete agreement.

"There are rainy days to come, Gary, and there are bright and sunny ones. Keeping well-tended cash on hand not only helps you cushion life's blows—it also helps take advantage of life's opportunities when they come around." Emily reached into her file, took out a publication entitled *A Home Buyer's Guide* and handed it to Gary. "Happy house hunting," she said with a smile.

For additional advice on financing and buying a home, as well as an enlightening analysis of buying versus renting, see the bonus chapter, "The Savvy Home-Buyer's Guide," on page 119.

CHAPTER 4

Secrets to Saving Smartly

Gary took Emily's advice to heart. After his meeting with her, Gary put the $100,000 in an online savings account he rarely accessed — a clever tactic, he thought, designed to keep the money out of sight, out of mind, and out of hand. He then went on a search for a nice house and a good mortgage. He eventually found both. A few months later, he was living in a completely refurnished mid-sized bungalow immersed in wedding plans.

After the wedding, Gary checked on his $100,000. It was safe and sound in his savings account, earning less than a whopping 1 percent interest.

Then it finally hit him. *One percent,* Gary thought. *This $100,000 is only earning one percent. That's not the number Emily used when she convinced me to set this money aside on my last visit.* Gary looked at some of the charts Emily gave him their last meeting. Sure enough, Emily had run all her examples with a 5 percent return. *Five percent,* Gary thought. *Where on earth was Emily getting 5 percent? Stocks? Mutual Funds? The Magic Kingdom?*

Gary had to solve the mystery. He set up another appointment and brought all the charts from their last meeting.

"Congratulations on your wedding, Gary," Emily said cheerfully as he walked in. "A married man. Wow. Seems only yesterday you were sitting in Ms. Johnson's math class."

"Yep," he replied with a disbelieving shake of his head as he put his charts on the table.

"Emily, when I was last here, just after Aunt Emma passed, you had talked to me about saving the $100,000 instead of buying the house for cash."

"Yes, I did."

"So, I was looking at the charts from our last meeting and saw that the examples we used all involved the money compounding at 5%. That money is now earning less than 1% in an online savings account. Where oh where did you get the 5% interest rate in these examples? Did you figure it would be in the stocks or bonds or fairyland…?"

Emily smiled before he went on. "I don't mind setting the money aside, but I'd rather see it earn the 5% we talked about, instead of the 1% I'm earning in my savings account — a rate that seems to decrease, and that's before taxes, every time I look at it."

Emily looked intently at Gary and took a sip of her tea. "Funny you should ask, Gary. Good question. I would have addressed it at our last meeting, but I was hitting you with so much already, I didn't want to confuse or overwhelm you."

"Good point. But I've had a chance to think about what we talked about. And I'm ready for the next step. I'm really curious where the 5 percent came from."

"And I'm going to tell you. But before I do that, I'd like to run a few numbers for you. Would that be okay?"

"I would expect nothing less, Emily. That's why I'm here."

Emily smiled and called up the Average vs. Actual Rates of Return calculator on her Truth Concepts software. She turned her screen for Gary to better see.

"So, you had asked about mutual funds," said Emily. "It's where many beginning investors put their money, and it can be a good place to start, especially if you're investing in no-load index funds. But there's something I need you to be aware of before going down this path."

"All righty," said Gary.

"Mutual funds generally advertise their *average* rate of return. Their average return can sometimes be in stark contrast to their *actual* rates of return, especially in shorter timeframes. So, it's important to know the difference. Let's run a scenario."

"Okay. Let's do it," answered Gary with a silly smile.

"Now, this is an extreme example, but just to make the point obvious. If you invested that $100,000 in a fund that advertised an average 25% return, you could double your money — earn a 100% return — the first year." Emily pointed to the Average vs. Actual calculator shown in Figure 17 on the next page spread.

"An excellent return. But say it was a volatile fund and it lost 50% of your money — entirely half — the second year." She pointed to the calculator (Figure 18 on the next page spread).

"This would bring you back to a 0% rate of return for those two years. That fund could still average a 25% return. The numbers are accurate: (100% + (50%) / 2 = 25%). But your effective return would be 0% — because doubling your money, and then halving it would give you a 0% gain, leaving you back where you started."

"Ummmmm....OK." Gary murmured. "But that seems like kind of an extreme example."

"It is," replied Emily, "but it's just to illustrate that *average*

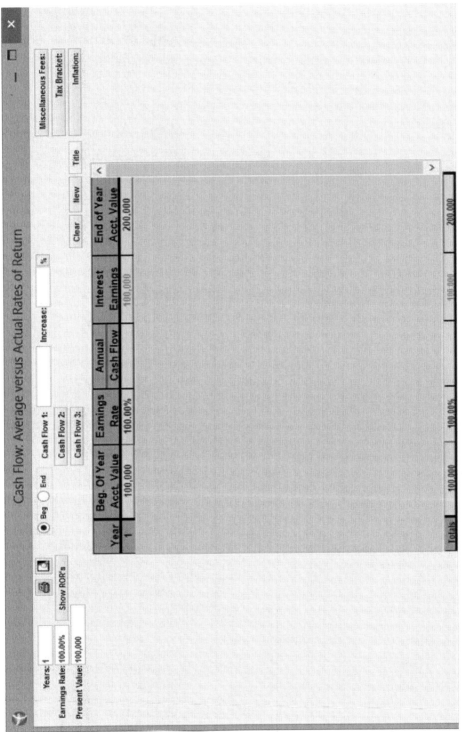

Figure 17

TruthConcepts.com

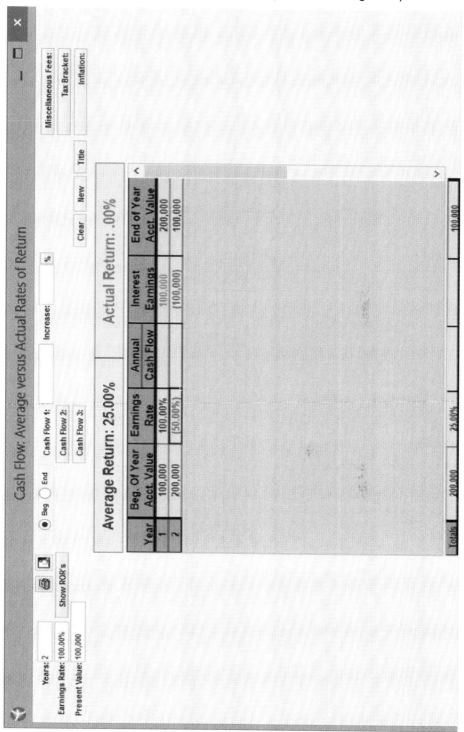

Figure 18

returns can be deceiving. Be sure you always check a fund's *actual* track record, the *actual* returns it's earned its investors, before putting your money in it."

Gary looked up from the screen. "OK. That sounds good. So, I guess mutual funds are it then, what you used when calculating a 5% return?"

"Well, not really," replied Emily. "But before we go into that, there's one more concept I'd like to explain to you. OK?"

"Okay."

"So, it's the idea that a high rate of return can make up for a paltry saving habit. In other words, people are always looking for the highest rate of return. But if you crunch the numbers, you see that *the amount saved* actually has a much bigger impact in creating wealth than a few percentage points increase or decrease in your earnings rate."

"Okay. Let's see the numbers."

"All righty. So, let's pull up the Maximum Potential calculator, shall we...? This calculates what your savings or investments look like in different scenarios."

"Sounds good," replied Gary.

Emily pulled up the Maximum Potential calculator and entered the following inputs in the top left Income Data fields:

Illustration Period:	35 Years
Annual Income:	$100,000
Annual Income Increase:	4%
Annual Earnings Rate:	5%

Up popped the chart in Figure 19 on the opposite page.

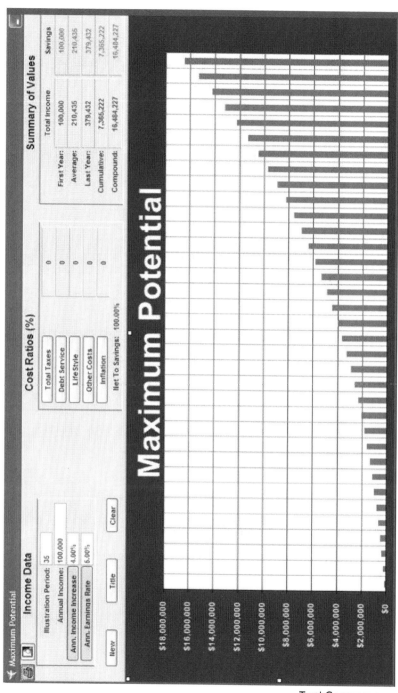

TruthConcepts.com

Figure 19

"Now," Emily went on, "this example pretends you have no costs, because it shows the result of investing the *entirety* of your $100,000 income each year. In the top right Summary of Values section, the bottom-most field, you'll see this scenario yields $16 million over 35 years. But now, let's start inputting the costs of an actual human life in the middle Cost Ratio section.

"In fact, let's start straight away with taxes at 40%. That's including income tax, sales tax, all of the tax you pay." Emily entered 40% in the Total Taxes field in the Cost Ratios section in the middle of the calculator, Figure 20 (opposite page).

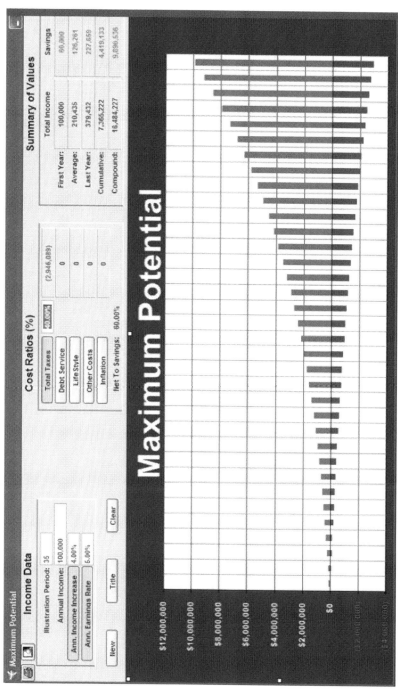

TruthConcepts.com

Figure 20

"Now, that's if we *only* paid taxes and saved."

"Taxes and savings. Yes, I see that," said Gary.

"All right. Let's add 34% in debt service because, unfortunately, most Americans are swimming in debt." (Figure 21 below.)

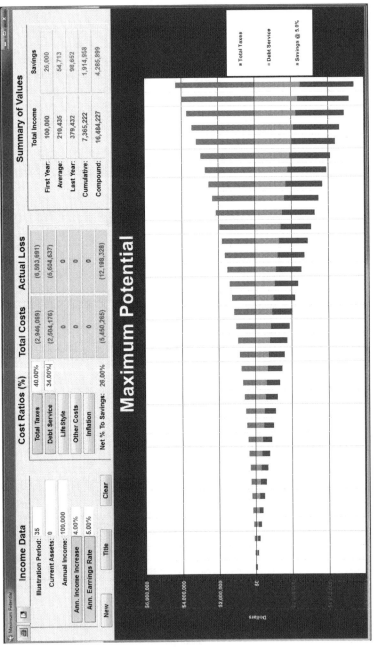

Figure 21

"That brings our savings down to $4.2 million.

"Then, let's enter Life Style, which is just ordinary, recurring living expenses, at 23%. We'll also enter Other Costs, perhaps gifts and vacations, at 1%. (Figure 22 below.)

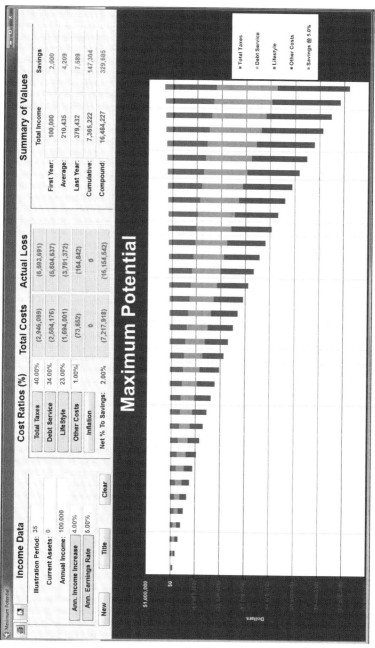

Figure 22

"As you can see, if we account for all the money at these percentages, with the entire remainder going into savings, this puts our savings amount after 35 years at a whopping $329,685, and our savings rate at a mere 2%."

"Ouch," said Gary, "Even for me, that doesn't sound like much, especially 35 years in the future. But are those percentages realistic? I mean, 34% in debt service and 40% in taxes?"

"I'm afraid they are, Gary, though it gives me no joy to say it. Most Americans are blowing all the money they make — and then some — even those with higher incomes. At least in this example this person is saving 2%. That's something, and more than many are saving."

"Mmmmm. OK. But if that's the case, then *shouldn't* we look for the highest earnings rate we can get? I mean, if we're all hardly saving anything, than shouldn't we get the highest earnings rate possible?"

"Good point. Let's see. Let's double the Annual Earnings Rate in the bottom field of the upper left Income Data section. Let's change it from 5% to 10%."

Emily entered the new earnings rate and hit return. The chart in Figure 23 (opposite page) appeared.

"As you can see, doubling your earnings rate from 5% to 10%, without adjusting any other costs or inputs, brings the amount saved up to $885,733. It's more money, for sure. It's something."

"Well, it's something," said Gary, "but I don't think it will be enough to live on, especially so far in the future. So, that's the result of doubling my rate of return from 5% to 10%? It actually doesn't seem like that much."

"No, it's not," said Emily. "But let's try another approach. Let's tinker with the costs, adjusting the values in the middle Cost Ratios

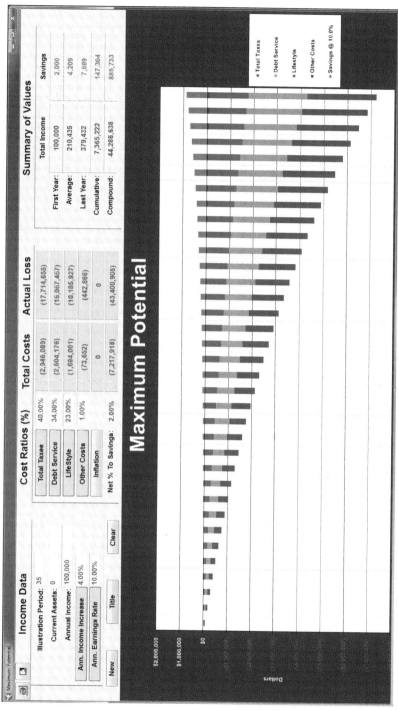

Figure 23

TruthConcepts.com

section. Let's reduce those costs while putting the resulting savings into the savings pile, OK?"

"Sounds good."

"All right, then," said Emily. "So let's bring the Annual Earnings Rate in the upper left corner back down to 5%. Then, let's decrease the cost inputs in the middle Cost Ratios section. Say we moved assets around a bit and reduced our tax liability. If our current tax liability is 40%, and we reduced that 40% by 10% (40 / 10% = 4), our new tax liability percentage would be 36%, a nice reduction. Let's see what that would do." (See Figure 24, opposite page.)

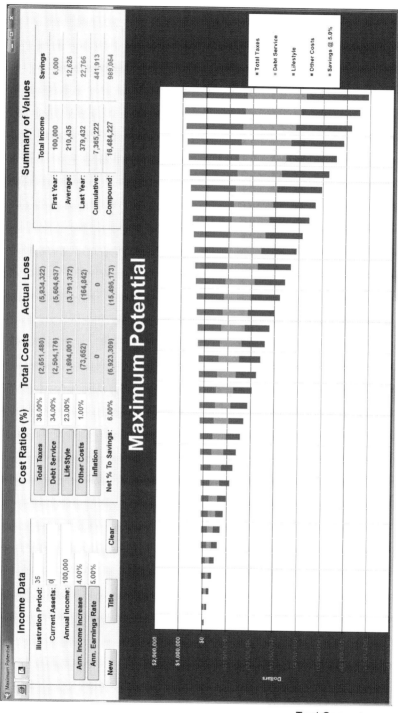

Figure 24

TruthConcepts.com

"Well, just bringing the tax liability down from 40% to 36%, and putting the difference in savings, increases the amount saved from $329,685 to $989,054."

"Holy moly. Now that's a big change."

"It sure is," said Emily. "But watch this. Let's tackle that debt. Let's reduce our debt service by only 10% — so, 10% of 34% equals 3.4%. Subtract that from the original 34% number, and that leaves you with 30.6%. Let's calculate our savings with this new 30.6% number in the debt service field and see how that affects our result." (See Figure 25, opposite page.)

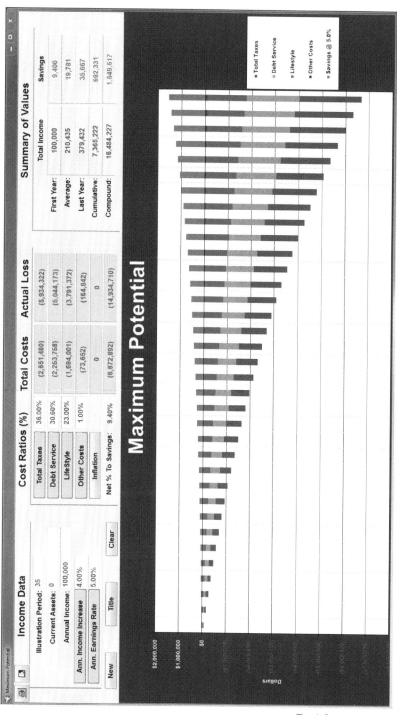

Figure 25

TruthConcepts.com

"That raises our end result up from \$989,054 to more than \$1.5 million — and brings our savings rate up to 9.4%."

"Wow. \$1.5 million. Now that's some serious money," said Gary.

"It is," said Emily. "And it illustrates my point. Everyone's clamoring for a better return, the best possible interest rate, going to the wall for a one, two, or three percent rate increase. What I'm trying to emphasize is that it's the *amount* saved, not a few points interest rate here or there, over your lifetime, that what will make the big difference in the end.

Emily leaned back to see if Gary had absorbed this point properly.

Gary looked up. "Okay, I got it Emily. What you're saying is focus on your *savings* rate, the *amount* of money you save over time, not so much the interest rate earned on that savings."

"Exactly. I'm trying to get you in the habit of saving. You need to flex that muscle, Gary. You need to flex it enough to make it part of your autonomic nervous system. Because once it becomes that, not only will saving not feel like such a burden, it will feel strange *not* to do it."

"A-ha."

"Have you heard of the book, *The Richest Man in Babylon*?"

"No. I have not," responded Gary.

Emily reached under her desk and pulled out a copy. "Well, here." She handed the book over to Gary. "This book is for you to keep. Just like the savings portion of your earnings. Ten percent of all you earn is yours to keep. Or, more specifically, spend nine of every ten gold coins you receive. One gold coin is to go to savings."

Gary took the book. "Thanks, Emily. I will read this. I get the point you're trying to make. Develop a habit of saving, rain or shine. One gold coin out of every ten, as you say." Gary smiled and fanned the pages of the book.

"Yup. That's the point. You're a good student, Gary."

Emily took another sip of tea, folded her hands, and leaned back. She smiled at Gary, and they sat in silence for a minute. Then, as the silence lingered, Emily glanced off to the side, wondering if she had missed something.

"Um, Emily."

"Yes?"

"You still haven't told me where the 5% earnings rate came from."

"Oh." Emily laughed." She smiled and animatedly turned her chair to grab another small book from behind her desk. "Well, Gary, *that* is from a financial instrument I recommend highly to many of my clients. It's a savings vehicle called a whole life insurance policy."

"Were you planning on telling me about this, Ms. Emily?"

"I was, Mr. Gary. But, before I did that, I wanted to make sure your emergency fund was fully stocked. The vehicle I'm talking about is known as the cash value. It's part of a whole life insurance policy. It's a great place to store cash — like I said, it's a savings vehicle — *after* your emergency funds are up and fully operational."

"OK. Well, I'm doing pretty well in that department. Could I learn a little more about this?"

"Of course," Emily continued, "the cash value portion of a whole life policy earns a higher interest rate than your ordinary savings account. Actually, let me clarify that.

"Whole life companies are usually *mutual* companies, which means they don't pay an interest rate but instead distribute 100 percent of their profits as dividends to their policyholders each year. We often express those dividends as a percentage, so as to create a fair comparison between whole life and other savings vehicles.

"Right now, the cash value component of a whole life policy pays three to five percent per year. Sometimes, it can be more."

"Huh. So, I like 3 percent to 5 percent. It's certainly better than the 1 percent or less I'm earning in my savings. But didn't you just get through saying how your earnings rate is less important than the amount you save?"

"A-ha. Can't get anything by you, can I?" Emily laughed. "I did just say that. And it's true. That's one reason we always set up policies with something called a PUA rider — that stands for 'Paid-Up Additions.' PUAs allow you to increase the amount you're saving. Plus, the rider helps make your policy flexible so that you have an option to save extra cash in the policy when you are able.

"And there are other factors to consider with cash value whole life. One specifically is that you can't lose your principal, the original money you placed into the policy, as you can in stocks or mutual funds. Another is that the dividends you earn are *not* taxed. That's huge, Gary, especially when dealing with larger sums of money."

"Yeah."

"And on top of that, you can borrow against any cash value you build up at pretty nominal rates. That can come in really handy later in life."

"I see."

"Yep. And then, of course, there's the life insurance component, which stays in force for the entirety of your life, not just a ten- or twenty- or thirty-year term. And the premiums also stay level for your entire life. You don't have to renew down the road at astronomical, unaffordable, and sometimes unattainable premiums. Whatever you sign on to at the time you buy the policy is your premium for life. And often, that premium only needs to be paid for seven to twenty years."

"Wow. So, I should sign up, don't you think...?"

"Yes, as long as you are confident you can save a consistent amount, annually or monthly, for at least a few years. Here's a great little book that explains more about it. It's called *Live Your Life Insurance*. Take a look at it." Emily handed Gary the book. "Whole life can be a great tool, but it's also quite a commitment, so I want you to be ready for it.

"OK. That sounds like a plan," answered Gary.

Gary looked down at the book in his hand. "Thanks Emily. For everything." He smacked the paperback down on the desk as he rose from his chair. "And I'll be back. I'll bring my wife, and we can talk about this new possibility."

Emily smiled as she waved back. "I'm counting on it."

CHAPTER 5

Leveraging Your Cash Value

Things had improved dramatically for Gary over the years. He had worked out a deal to buy the Vaipanzo's construction company after they retired, and the business was going well. But in many ways, he was still trading time for money. What he recognized he needed was "passive" income—money being made without direct correlation to his time, money being made while he was sleeping or on vacation.

Through talking about his desire for passive income with other people, Gary realized that he wanted to explore real estate investing. After all, being in construction, he already understood the physical aspect of homes. Now he just needed an understanding of the financial side of real estate investing.

"Emily!" Gary said as he walked into her office. The two shook hands.

"Have a seat, Gary," she replied, gesturing to one of the chairs in front of her desk. "How have things been?"

"I'd say pretty good. Business is solid; personal life is going well. Really can't complain."

"Nice," Emily replied. "It's been great to watch you grow over all these years."

"Well, you've certainly been there for that. And I'm grateful. In fact, that's a good segue into why I'm here. I'm looking to move into passive income, and I'm thinking about real estate."

"There are a lot of good reasons to invest." She took a sip of the steaming tea she'd been enjoying, which nicely offset the chilly January view outside her window.

"I agree, and I'm really looking to make use of the cash value I have in my whole-life policy. It's gotten to be a pretty good chunk of change."

"It certainly has," she agreed, glancing at the screen on her laptop. "I'd pulled up the numbers earlier. You're in a great position to use this for real estate."

"All right. That's what I wanted to hear!" Gary leaned forward with enthusiasm. "So, you're my guru. What do I need to know? Where do we go from here?"

"Ha! Well, I don't know about guru, but I'm happy to get you going with the right steps." She closed the lid on her laptop. "And for once, I don't need to show you a bunch of charts and graphs."

"Sounds good," Gary said as he realized he still had his jacket on. He took it off as Emily started to share her first point.

"The biggest thing to remind you is that you're *not* borrowing your own money. That cash value you have growing and accruing interest, that doesn't get touched. And that's great, because it will continue to grow while you *borrow against it*." She emphasized each of those last three words with a tap of her finger on her desktop.

"So, you mean my cash value is just collateral?"

"Exactly. The life insurance company loans you the money with your cash account as security."

"Well then," Gary said, "why wouldn't I just get a loan at my bank or elsewhere?"

"You could, but there are two great things about these loans versus typical loans—one, there's no qualification process, and two, you can determine your own payback structure. Pay it back as slowly or quickly as you'd like, even with irregular payments and amounts. This flexibility can be a huge advantage over a traditional loan."

"Ah, right… I remember some of this from what you'd taught me before. Really great to hear again," Gary said with a nod of satisfaction. "I don't suppose you're gonna tell me these are zero-interest loans, right?"

"Yeah, right!" Emily laughed. "Contrary to popular request, life insurance companies still insist on making money off their loans. So no luck there. But when you get to a property you have your eye on, we'll see what makes the most sense, using the Truth Concepts real estate calculator including your best rate options from other financing. But while we're at it, let's tackle one interest issue that's specific to cash-value loans."

"I'm ready," Gary said, as Emily finished the last of her tea and composed her thoughts to start into this tricky area.

"Okay. There's a concept called 'direct recognition,' which affects the interest rate you pay on the loan as well as the interest your collateralized portion of your cash account earns during your loan term. In a *non-direct recognition* company, it's simple—your loan has no effect on the interest rate you earn. However, your life insurance company uses *direct recognition*."

"Since I'm guessing you're going to say my interest rate is affected, why do I have a direct-recognition company?"

"Perfect. Now, back to the point at hand." She smiled. "In a direct-recognition company like yours, the interest rate you earn on the collateralized portion of your cash account will usually be different than the remainder of your cash account. Does that make sense?"

"I'm pretty sure. So in the case of my money…?"

"Your cash value right now is just a tad under $112,000. So, if you took a $32,000 loan against it, that would mean $32,000 of your account is collateralized, while $80,000 isn't, and each amount will likely be earning a different rate."

"Ah, I see."

"And," Emily quickly interjected, "the effect can be positive or negative. In other words, either rate could be higher… it just depends on the state of the company's dividends at the time of your loan. So, I know it sounds weird, but in some cases, the collateralized portion of your cash account could actually earn more than the rest of your cash account." Gary nodded his head for a few moments, letting that sink in.

"All right," he said. "So the main takeaway here is that I'll be earning two different interest rates on my cash value during the time of my loan."

"Correct—one for the amount that's collateralized and one for the amount that's not."

"But what about the interest rate on the loan itself?"

"Well," she said, sipping her tea, "that's just like any other loan; you'll be paying whatever the rate is at the time. Or the fixed rate if your company charges that."

"Is it usually competitive?"

"It can be, especially when you factor in the flexibility of the loan."

"Sounds good," he said. "Now, I've just got to find that great property and great deal, and then we can dive into your Truth Concepts Calculator yet again."

"Absolutely. But let me just share a couple more things with you before you go."

"I'm all ears." He remembered his tea and enjoyed a sip.

"Remember how we set your policy up with the capability for Paid-Up Additions, or PUAs? At times in the past, you've utilized this option by paying over and above your premium when you had extra cash you could store in your policy. And when you take loans against your policy, you can choose to pay back at a rate higher than what they are charging on a loan, which is one way of taking advantage of the PUA rider. For instance, you can pay a loan back at 9 percent instead of 6 percent, and that extra portion of your payment becomes your PUA. The key point is that about 95 percent of your PUA goes toward your cash account while the rest increases your death benefit. And as you know, it's a great idea to add to your cash account as often as you can — so you may as well make the most of it."

"Wow," Gary said. "I can see that. So, it sounds like, depending on the return on investment I project from my investment property, it might be wise to take advantage of this PUA, right?"

"Yeah. This is often ideal with real estate, where you can have a significant return that makes paying extra toward a PUA more than feasible."

"Right."

"So, does all this make sense?" she asked. "Any questions?"

"Nope. I think I'm all clear. Emily, you've done it again," Gary said, shaking his head in amazement at her sage advice. "I can't thank you enough. Now I'm really excited to get going on a real estate deal."

"My pleasure," she replied. "You know I'm behind you all the way. You're my longest-time client. It's been tremendous to watch you evolve as you have."

"Onward and upward!" he said, raising his mug and taking another drink of his tea. "I have a feeling I'll be back to you really soon to crunch the numbers on a deal." Emily stood to walk him out of the office.

"I have no doubt, Gary. I have no doubt."

CHAPTER 6

Profitable Real Estate Investing

It wasn't long before Gary was back in Emily's office with a real estate deal he was truly excited about. She could tell the moment he walked in, not to mention that her assistant had said he was eager for the first appointment he could get.

"Well, aren't you all a-buzz!" Emily said as Gary put down his black leather binder with his property-search results.

"You can tell?" he said with mock surprise.

"Let's just say, you wear your money on your sleeve."

"Good one!"

"So, whatcha got?" she said, peering toward the binder as he pulled out a blue folder.

"Well, first... thank you very much for the referral to Dianne. She's a great real estate agent, obviously knows her stuff, and is a tremendous help."

"You're welcome, Gary. Dianne's been great to me over the years, both for my own real estate deals as well as my clients'. She knows the money side, so I know she's going to pick great properties."

"As she did for me! But this one is really perfect. You both had said it would be smart to find a place to rent out as corporate housing since so many business travelers come and go here. And this is it." He fingered over the listing sheet with the details for Emily to see.

"Wow. Only five miles from the airport. That's big."

"Yeah, and I've got a guy I know who runs a car service, so I can even offer that as a perk—free executive sedan service to and from the airport." Gary's enthusiasm filled the room.

"It looks like there's some fixer-upper stuff to do," she said.

"No big deal for me. That's my specialty."

"Exactly," she continued, "looks fabulous to me. I'd bet you could easily get $600 weekly from this."

"Try $700-800. Dianne said I could expect that, gross."

"Nice!" Emily replied as Gary nodded with a smile. She started tapping away at her keyboard, and he knew she was bringing up her Truth Concepts software. "The Truth Concepts software has a nifty little Real Estate Analysis Calculator to forecast your rate of return on an investment property." Emily turned the monitor so Gary could see. "It's only a one-page form, so it's really quick and easy."

"Let's do it!"

"Okay," she started, pointing at the screen shown in Figure 26. "Let's look at the top left under 'Property Information.' We'll set the property value and sales price at $200,000, just to be conservative; let's assume they'll take no less than they're asking. Now, we'll add in $5,000 for closing costs. Then, let's set the land value at $35,000 and house value at $165,000. We do this because you can only deduct depreciation from your taxes for the structure, so let's figure the land value separately."

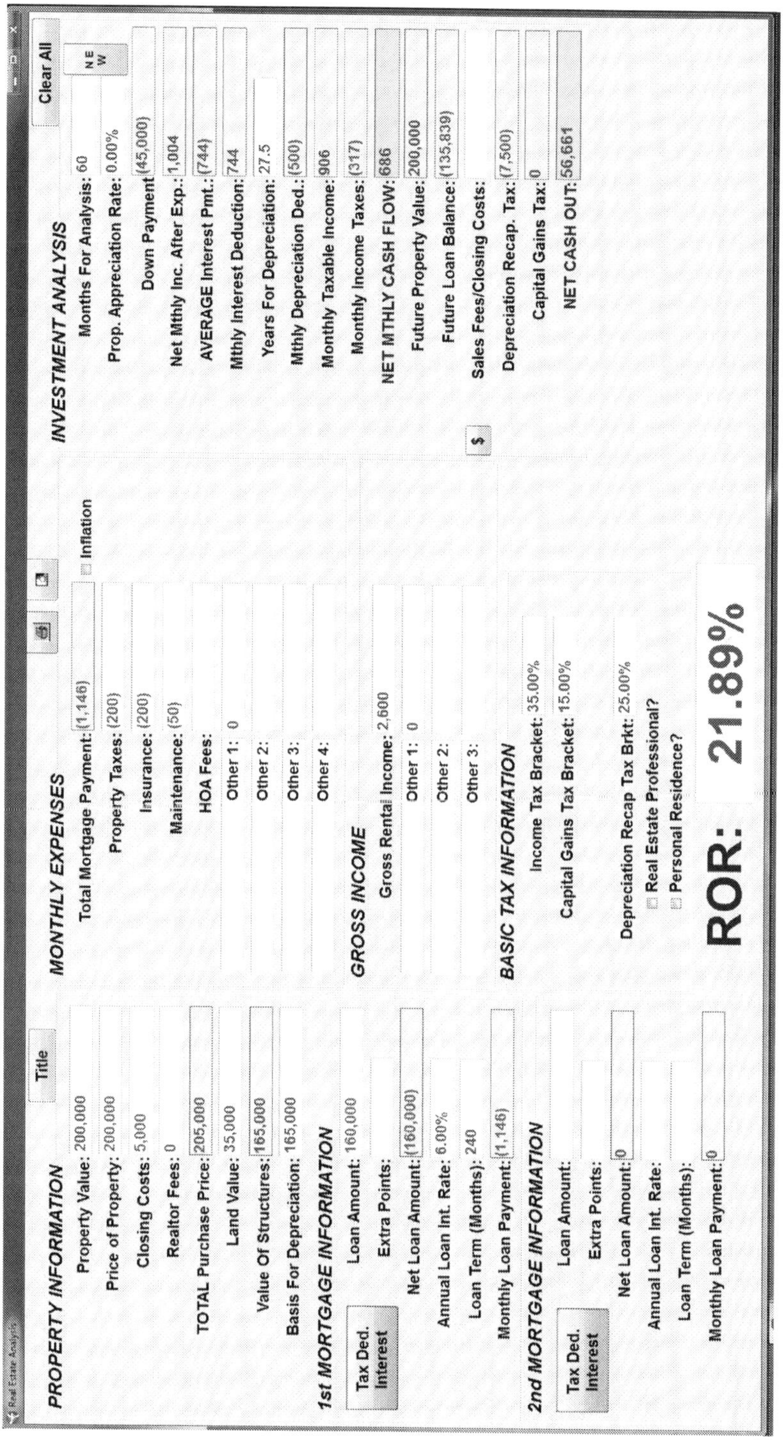
Real Estate Analysis
Title
Clear All
PROPERTY INFORMATION
Property Value: 200,000
Price of Property: 200,000
Closing Costs: 5,000
Realtor Fees: 0
TOTAL Purchase Price: 205,000
Land Value: 35,000
Value Of Structures: 165,000
Basis For Depreciation: 165,000
1st MORTGAGE INFORMATION
Tax Ded. Interest
Loan Amount: 160,000
Extra Points:
Net Loan Amount: (160,000)
Annual Loan Int. Rate: 6.00%
Loan Term (Months): 240
Monthly Loan Payment: (1,146)
2nd MORTGAGE INFORMATION
Tax Ded. Interest
Loan Amount:
Extra Points:
Net Loan Amount: 0
Annual Loan Int. Rate:
Loan Term (Months):
Monthly Loan Payment: 0
MONTHLY EXPENSES
Inflation
Total Mortgage Payment: (1,146)
Property Taxes: (200)
Insurance: (200)
Maintenance: (50)
HOA Fees:
Other 1: 0
Other 2:
Other 3:
Other 4:
GROSS INCOME
Gross Rental Income: 2,600
Other 1: 0
Other 2:
Other 3:
BASIC TAX INFORMATION
Income Tax Bracket: 35.00%
Capital Gains Tax Bracket: 15.00%
Depreciation Recap Tax Brkt: 25.00%
Real Estate Professional?
Personal Residence?
ROR: 21.89%
INVESTMENT ANALYSIS
NEW
Months For Analysis: 60
Prop. Appreciation Rate: 0.00%
Down Payment: (45,000)
Net Mthly Inc. After Exp.: 1,004
AVERAGE Interest Pmt.: (744)
Mthly Interest Deduction: 744
Years For Depreciation: 27.5
Mthly Depreciation Ded.: (500)
Monthly Taxable Income: 906
Monthly Income Taxes: (317)
NET MTHLY CASH FLOW: 686
Future Property Value: 200,000
Future Loan Balance: (135,839)
Sales Fees/Closing Costs:
$
Depreciation Recap. Tax: (7,500)
Capital Gains Tax: 0
NET CASH OUT: 56,661

TruthConcepts.com

Figure 26

"Okay. Got it," Gary said.

"It's just an estimate, but I'm sure it'll be close enough for our purposes. Now, just below that, under the '1ˢᵗ Mortgage Information' section, we'll enter the details of the mortgage. As you can see, the last field in that section will calculate the monthly mortgage loan payment."

"The red $1,146 per month at the bottom of that section?" Gary asked.

"Right." Emily then pointed to the middle column on the screen. "See here, under the 'Monthly Expenses' section? Your mortgage payment automatically shows up, but we still need to enter your monthly costs—property taxes at $200, insurance at $200, and maintenance at $50. And then, if you look below that, you'll see the 'Gross Income' section. Now, Dianne estimated that you could earn $700–800 gross per week from this property…" Emily trailed off to think for a moment. "But let's estimate low. So, in the Gross Rental Income field, let's enter $2,600 per month. This takes into account some weeks the property sits vacant."

"I'm with you. She said it's not uncommon to have eight to ten weeks a year it'll sit empty."

"Exactly, Gary." Emily then pointed below the 'Gross Income' field to the 'Basic Tax Information' section. "Here we'll set your income tax at 35 percent, capital gains at 15 percent, and depreciation recapture at 25 percent." She looked to Gary to be sure he got it.

"No problem there," he said, "but the capital gains… I was planning on doing a Starker Exchange down the road."

"That's great. But we want to be sure this deal stands on its own, without relying on that. Your circumstances might change, and besides, even with the Starker you'll eventually have to pay that tax in some form."

"Starker" Exchange:

Under Section 1031 of the United States Internal Revenue Code (26 U.S.C. § 1031), the exchange of certain types of property may defer the recognition of capital gains or losses due upon sale, and hence defer any capital gains taxes otherwise due.

From Wikipedia.org

"Okay, Emily. I gotcha."

"Now, here, Gary." She pointed to the Real Estate Professional box just below the tax fields. "If you log 750 hours or more of real estate work per year, you can write off your expenses against any regularly earned income in that year; otherwise, the losses will roll over."

"750's a lot. That's about 15 hours per week."

"Right, but a lot of activities qualify, so you'll want to coordinate with your accountant on this. And the IRS watches this closely, so be sure to nail down the requirements and keep excellent records of your activities and time."

"Yep. Will do."

"Now, we go to the final section on the right: 'Investment Analysis.' We're going to analyze this deal for five years, a 60-month time frame. Also, we're going with zero appreciation."

She caught the look on Gary's face without even glancing up. "I know, I know… everyone thinks their place is going to go up 10 percent a year or whatever. But let's just look at appreciation as gravy and see if this real estate investment stands on its own, purely from cash flow—because that's something you have more control over. You have no control over whether the property value will go up or down. So, for now, let's keep appreciation at zero."

"Fair enough. You keep me in reality check."

"That's right. Plus, this is Truth Concepts software, not Fantasy Concepts software." Gary laughed. "Okay," Emily said, "now we enter values in the last three fields below that—$45,000 for your down payment, 27.5 years for depreciation (which would be 39 years if it were a commercial building), and $12,000 for your sales fees and closing costs."

"I thought we already did closing costs."

"That was on your purchase," said Emily. "These are closing costs when you sell."

"Ah, gotcha."

"So, as you can see, Gary, at about the center of the right column—your Net Monthly Cash Flow for the analysis period of five years would be $686, and, once you sold, your Net Cash Out would be $56,661.

And this gives us the giant number in the bottom center of the calculator—you can't miss it—the annual rate of return, ROR. Your ROR would be 21.89 percent on those initial dollars you invested in the property in the first place."

"Not bad!"

"Now," Emily said, "since I know you'd love some appreciation, as we all would, let's see how things look with a modest 4 percent appreciation rate." She pointed out the 'Prop. Appreciation Rate' field toward the top of the right-hand column.

Gary then saw that his ROR had now gone up to 29.22 percent [Figure 27]. "And," Emily continued, "you'll see here, under 'Net Cash Out' in the bottom right, that would go up tremendously—to $94,230."

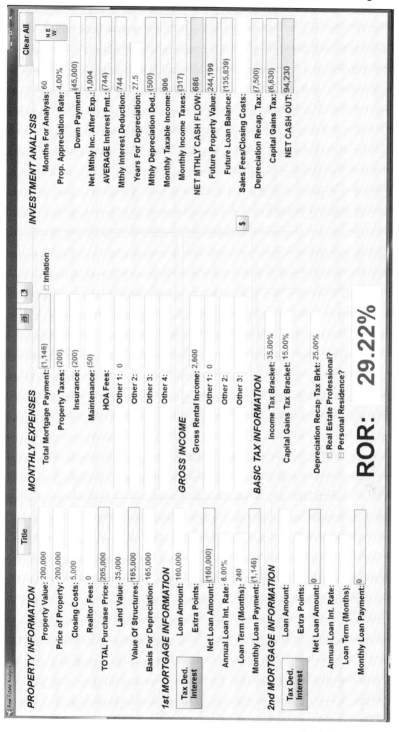

Figure 27

TruthConcepts.com

"Now we're talkin'!"

"I thought you'd like that. But you wanna know what's even better? OPM: Other People's Money."

"Ah, yes... like borrowing against the cash value in my life insurance."

"Exactly. Because even though your cash flow goes down, since you have an additional loan payment to make each month, your ROR is much higher because it's based on the use of that *borrowed* money." She pointed to the screen [Figure 28] to show the ROR of 125 percent.

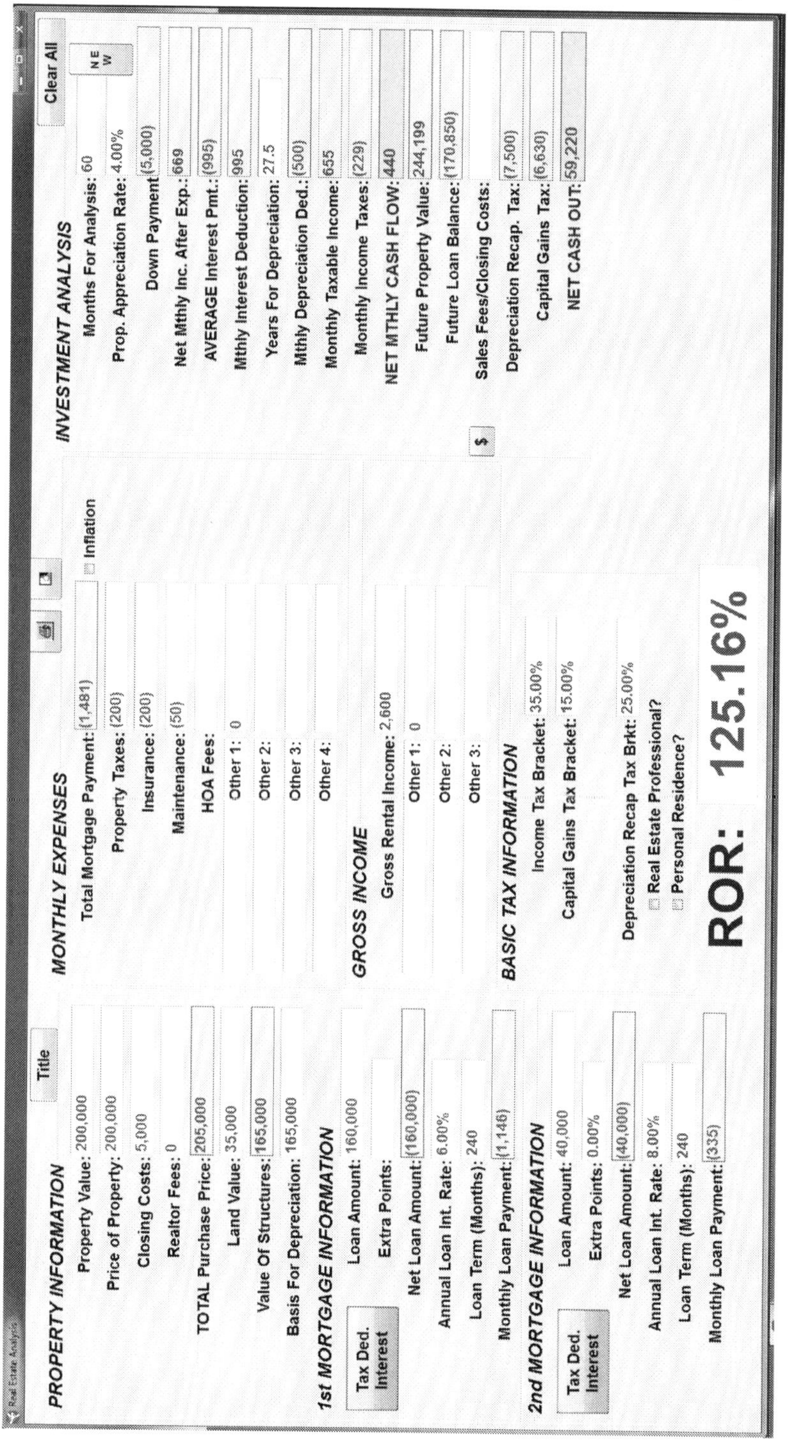

Real Estate Analysis

Title | | Inflation | | Clear All

PROPERTY INFORMATION

Property Value: 200,000
Price of Property: 200,000
Closing Costs: 5,000
Realtor Fees: 0
TOTAL Purchase Price: 205,000
Land Value: 35,000
Value Of Structures: 165,000
Basis For Depreciation: 165,000

1st MORTGAGE INFORMATION

Loan Amount: 160,000

Tax Ded. Interest

Extra Points:
Net Loan Amount: (160,000)
Annual Loan Int. Rate: 6.00%
Loan Term (Months): 240
Monthly Loan Payment: (1,146)

2nd MORTGAGE INFORMATION

Loan Amount: 40,000

Tax Ded. Interest

Extra Points: 0.00%
Net Loan Amount: (40,000)
Annual Loan Int. Rate: 8.00%
Loan Term (Months): 240
Monthly Loan Payment: (335)

MONTHLY EXPENSES

Total Mortgage Payment: (1,481)
Property Taxes: (200)
Insurance: (200)
Maintenance: (50)
HOA Fees:
Other 1: 0
Other 2:
Other 3:
Other 4:

GROSS INCOME

Gross Rental Income: 2,600
Other 1: 0
Other 2:
Other 3:

BASIC TAX INFORMATION

Income Tax Bracket: 35.00%
Capital Gains Tax Bracket: 15.00%

Depreciation Recap Tax Brkt: 25.00%
Real Estate Professional?
Personal Residence?

ROR: 125.16%

INVESTMENT ANALYSIS

Months For Analysis: 60
Prop. Appreciation Rate: 4.00%
Down Payment (5,000)
Net Mthly Inc. After Exp.: 669
AVERAGE Interest Pmt.: (995)
Mthly Interest Deduction: 995
Years For Depreciation: 27.5
Mthly Depreciation Ded.: (500)
Monthly Taxable Income: 655
Monthly Income Taxes: (229)
NET MTHLY CASH FLOW: 440
Future Property Value: 244,199
Future Loan Balance: (170,850)
Sales Fees/Closing Costs:
Depreciation Recap. Tax: (7,500)
Capital Gains Tax: (6,630)
NET CASH OUT: 59,220

$

Figure 28

TruthConcepts.com

"That's amazing."

"Yep, and that was based on a $40,000 second mortgage with an annual rate of 8 percent—the loan against your cash value." She showed him where that was input, under '2nd Mortgage Information' at the bottom-left corner of the calculator.

"Okay," Gary said. "I'm with you."

"Now, if you really want to get into some nitty-gritty on the financing, we can determine your ROR *specifically* for the $40,000 borrowed against your cash value." She pulled up the basic rate calculator. "We put in a present value of 8, which is the interest rate on your loan. Then, no payment, because we're only looking at the rate of return. Then, a future value of 29, which was the rate of return on your entire investment—the screen we saw before [Figure 27]. And then we put in one year, since we're talking about the *annual* rate of return. As you see, the ROR just on the $40,000 is 262.5 percent." [Figure 29]

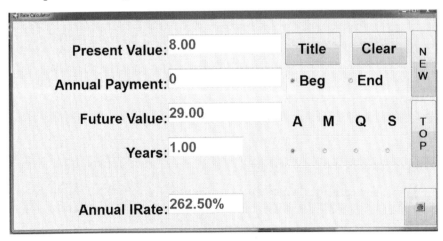

Figure 29

"Wow, that's almost unbelievable," said Gary.

"That's the value of being able to leverage against your savings and use OPM for investments," said Emily. "And I have to hand it to you, Gary. Most people don't have the patience to save. They start investing in mutual funds right away, trying to get a few extra percentage points. But you saved first. You built liquidity. Now you have the ability to start making some high quality investments. You should be very proud of yourself."

"Well, I am so very glad that you got me on the path for building up my cash-value account over all these years. That's certainly coming in handy right now."

"It sure is," Emily said. "As I almost always tell my clients, your best basic strategy is to use life insurance to *store* cash and real estate for cash *flow*. That combination meets the entire CLUE principle of Prosperity Economics—Control, Liquidity, Use, and Equity." (See next page.)

"Interesting," Gary said. "You often hear pundits talk about whole life insurance as an investment, but you're saying it's really savings."

"Exactly. The critics slam it based on being an investment vehicle, which it isn't—or shouldn't be. Unfortunately, there are enough people selling and promoting whole life as an investment to feed that criticism. But like I said, think of it as a place to store cash."

"All right," Gary agreed. "Now, I have just one more question."

"Shoot."

"If this property is such a good deal, then why am I still sitting here?"

"Well, yeah," Emily said with a laugh. "Get going!"

The CLUE Principle

C = Control

> You own it, you control it. It's your money, and it's not subject to market crashes or government restrictions.

L = Liquidity

> You can withdraw it, borrow against it, or simply let it grow. Liquid accounts can be easily accessed and don't typically fluctuate with the stock market.

U = Use

> Unlike accounts that accumulate dollars that cannot be touched for years to come, cash value accounts allow you to put your dollars to work.

E = Equity

> Just think real estate, because cash value insurance functions much the same way. Equity is leverageable; you can borrow against it while the underlying asset keeps on growing, unaffected by the debt.

CHAPTER 7

Life Settlements:
A True Alternative Investment

The modest house that Gary had purchased as an investment several years earlier and converted into a corporate rental had paid off. In fact, he parlayed that investment into multiple properties, including three other residences, two small apartment buildings, and a commercial duplex. Though he still owned his construction company, it no longer owned him—he'd put the right systems and people in place to manage things and considerably reduce his time commitment.

Gary had achieved a very comfortable level of wealth and was now looking for how to best increase his net worth in the coming year. Emily met him in the quiet corner of a café they both liked.

"How's the work going?" he asked.

"They're putting in the finishing touches," she said, "and it sounds like we might be open for business as early as next week." Emily's office townhouse was undergoing a top-to-bottom renovation by a company Gary had recommended. All the while, her employees had been working remotely and she was meeting clients in cafés and hotel lobbies. "So, again," she said, "thanks for connecting me with them, because they've done a great job keeping on schedule and within budget."

"Excellent. I'm looking forward to seeing the results. To your new office!" Gary lifted his coffee mug and clinked it with Emily's.

"So, my friend," she said. "You're looking to take it up a notch, huh?"

"Yep. You said once I was solidly where I'm at, we should talk." He looked around to make sure no one was within earshot.

"Well, right. For what I've had in mind for you, you needed to hit a million-dollar liquid net worth. And of course, I wanted you to be safely past that. Basically, this puts you in a position to be an 'accredited' investor. Until now, you've been faithfully funding your life insurance, your real estate, and your other smaller investments—and now you're ready for the big kahuna."

"Ha! You're funny," he said. "Okay, what are we talking about here?"

"Life settlements," she answered.

"Okay. That's a new one for me."

"It's certainly not unknown," she paused for a bite of her Danish, "but it's not talked about much because, like I said, it's only available to people with a million-plus net worth. It's not like you're going to hear much about it on a cable-TV finance show."

"Okay. Like you've always said, if you do what everyone else is doing, you'll get what everyone else is getting."

"Yep. My dad always said that. So, anyhow, here's the deal with life settlements: You purchase someone else's life insurance policy as an investment."

"Hmmm," Gary said.

"The money can come from your earnings or your IRA funds, and the 'someone else' is typically a person in his or her mid-80s who wants to sell his life insurance policy for cash today."

"Sounds like the person wouldn't have too many years left," Gary said, "so why would they do that?"

"Well, there can be many reasons, but the bottom line is that their policy beneficiaries don't need the death benefit, and they themselves need the money for their remaining years."

"Oh, so for example, the policyholder's spouse has already died, their kids don't really need the benefit, and the policyholder needs to go into an assisted-living home. You mean like that?"

"Exactly. That's one scenario. They need cash now, and sadly, a person's final years can cost a lot of money. A recent example is a woman in her 80s who didn't want the death benefit and didn't want to keep paying premiums. So, by selling her policy—which had a $1,000,000 death benefit and $400,000 of cash built up—she got $500,000 in immediate money as well as the money saved by not paying the premiums each month. That put her ahead of the game.

"So, you're saying I could've paid her the $500,000 to become the beneficiary of a $1,000,000 policy?"

"Well, technically, it's done through a life-settlement company, which does the purchasing, takes over the premiums, and becomes the beneficiary—but yes, you would put up your money and then receive the proportionate death benefit."

"That sounds kinda morbid," Gary said, wincing a little. "Basically, these life-settlement companies are banking on someone dying, and sooner rather than later because of the premiums they take over."

"I know it sounds odd, but remember, the seller gets more money than they would have if they'd cancelled the policy. Plus, they typically aren't solicited; they usually come to the life settlement company through their attorneys or accountants. The bottom line is, it's simply become more prevalent now that people are living longer and finding they need that money while they're alive—health care and assisted living can be unaffordable otherwise. So, while it feels morbid, it's really a win-win. You're helping people to be more comfortable in their final years. In return, you have a great investment."

"Wow… interesting. So, what are we talking about in terms of returns?"

"Well, let's look at an example," Emily said as she flipped open her laptop computer and fired up her Truth Concepts software. "Let's say a woman is selling her policy for $2 million—which is done through a life-settlement company."

"The company sets the price?" Gary asked.

"Not really. It's fluid. One company may offer more or less than another, and ultimately the policyholder decides."

"Okay, like basically selling anything."

"Right. So, the policy is being sold for $2 million, and you want to put in 1 percent on that deal. The death benefit, in return, is $4 million. So, to invest in 1 percent of a $2 million policy would cost you $20,000. Your return, consequently, would be $40,000 (1 percent of $4 million) when the woman passes away."

"Sounds straightforward," Gary said. "And she has the $2 million to live on for however long?"

"Yes, and that could be a lump sum for her, an annuity, or a number of other options."

"Gotcha."

"Now, the complication comes in the unknown factor—her remaining years. She could live another five or ten years, for all you know. And that, of course, greatly affects your rate of return. You would still ultimately get the $40,000, but as you know, over time, your return on your initial investment, or the rate of return—ROR—would decrease. This only comes into play when comparing a life settlement option with other investment opportunities, but it's still important to know. Nevertheless, you typically buy into a policy from someone with a life expectancy of two to seven years, which is what I recommend."

"Hmm… still seems more like a gamble."

"Well," Emily replied, "all investments, by nature, are gambles. They all carry a risk. That's the principal difference between savings and investments. But like all investments, we can assess and mitigate risk. Life-settlement companies look at life-expectancy tables and the individual medical specifics to assess the risks."

"So, when they buy the policy they know that it's an 85-year-old guy with a heart condition or whatever."

"Right. And really, it's no different than when a person gets life insurance to start with—the company checks out all your medical records and sometimes does an exam."

"Yep," Gary said. "Been there, done that."

"But in the end, no one really knows with certainty how many years we have left. George Burns smoked cigars and lived to 100. I know someone who had stage-four lung cancer and was gone within two months, while someone else I know has survived stage-four lung cancer for many years now. So, often what's helpful to do is to calculate returns for a variety of life-expectancy scenarios—to better understand what we're getting into. This is done with a simple rate calculator."

Emily moved her coffee so Gary could lean over to see the computer. She brought up the basic rate calculator and entered the values for the example they'd discussed—a present value of $20,000 (Gary's investment), an annual payment of $0, and a future value of $40,000 (Gary's ultimate return). The only variable that changed in the calculation was the remaining projected years of the policy-holder's life. In this case, the projection was based on an 85-year-old person with a life expectancy of 92.

As shown in Figure 30 below, if the person lived only another two years, Gary's ROR would be 41.42 percent. With each year, however, the ROR decreases from 18.92 percent at four years [Figure 31] to 10.41 percent if the policyholder were to live to her full life expectancy of age 92, seven more years [Figure 32, opposite page].

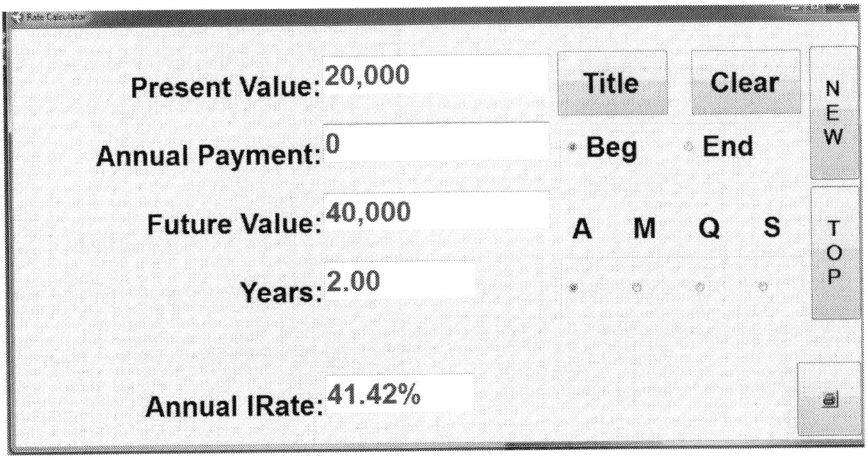

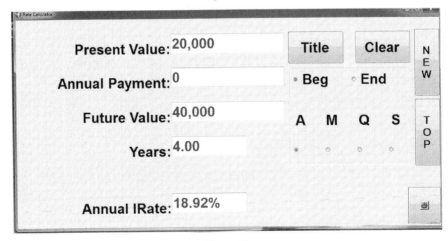

Figure 30

Figure 31

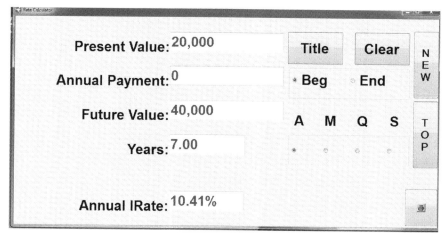

Figure 32

"Those are excellent returns," Gary said, "considering that this would be passive investing, I assume."

"Yes, Gary, I thought you'd appreciate that."

"You have no idea! I'm not sure I'll know what to do with myself if I'm not fixing up property, but I'd sure like to find out!"

Emily laughed.

"Now, are there any ongoing premium payments?" Gary asked.

"You can avoid having to pay those premiums by owning a policy *inside a fund* of settlements. It's kind of similar to a mutual fund in that it's a pool of investment money spread across many, many policies. And because of this, when someone lives past their life expectancy, the fund continues to pay the premiums with their reserves."

"Okay," Gary said. "I get it. And you think this is the route I should go?"

"I do, based on all we've discussed of your goals and where you are financially. As with any investment, this isn't right for everyone—even if the person had the required million-dollar net worth. But for your situation, I do think it's the right move."

"And," Gary started, pausing as the thought fully formed in his mind, "this life-settlement thing sounds like something I could do down the road if necessary, selling my policy at some point in the future."

"It's possible," Emily agreed. "But quite a bit down the road for you, I think. The only time a younger person would ever consider settling his policy is if he were diagnosed with a terminal illness, needed the cash—probably for medical expenses—and there was no one who absolutely needed the death benefit."

"Well, thank goodness," Gary said, knocking on the wood of the table, "I'm not in that situation. Just had my annual physical a couple weeks ago, in fact, and all is good."

And with that, the two—longtime advisor and client—clinked their coffee mugs to their mutual health, happiness, and prosperity.

* * * * * * * *

While Emily and Gary are fictional characters, Prosperity Economics helps real people build sustainable wealth using timeless principles, savvy strategies, and proven financial vehicles. Prosperity Economics also looks at your money holistically, weighing opportunity costs and seeing the big picture of how wealth is built.

Bonus Chapter:
The Savvy Home-Buyer's Guide

There's a lot of advice out there about buying homes and getting mortgages. Some of it is good and some of it is deeply flawed. In this guide, our focus is on how to buy a house that helps you build long-term wealth, not to provide detailed real estate advice.

Renting Versus Buying

In most cases, it makes more economic sense to be a homeowner in the long run. Studies and census bureau reports reveal that home buyers are better off than renters, with average net worths many times higher than renters. Information from the Federal Reserve indicates that home owners have net worths that average *36 times* higher than renters.

While you can argue that wealthier people are more likely to own homes, the data also shows that when other factors are the considered—such as income, age, race, and location—almost nothing raises a person's level of wealth more than home ownership! Most people cannot afford to purchase a home free and clear, and even if they can, it may not be the best decision. Yet by simply making mortgage payments over the term of a mortgage, a home buyer ends up with a valuable asset they can leverage for other investments, rent out for cash flow, or sell for cash.

Homeowners are consistently wealthier than renters — even with mortgages and home maintenance to worry about — because of one simple fact: It's difficult to build wealth when throwing money down "the rent drain." And just as the homeowner's house tends to appreciate over time along with inflation, so does the renter's rent. Using an appreciation rate of 4 percent, we see that the rent would increase a surprising 42 percent in just a decade — from a payment of $1,000 to $1,423 per month:

Ten years of renting at 4 percent inflation:

Year 1: $1,000/mo	Year 6: $1217
Year 2: $1040	Year 7: $1265
Year 3: $1082	Year 8: $1316
Year 4: $1125	Year 9: $1369
Year 5: $1170	Year 10: $1423

What about 30 years of renting? Your $1,000 rent payment will more than TRIPLE to a whopping $3,119! Sound unrealistic? From Portland, Oregon to Portland, Maine, cities are reporting rents increasing at least this quickly. See how the payment continues to climb over the next 20 years at the same 4 percent inflation:

Year 11: $1,480/mo	Year 16: $1801	Year 21: $2191	Year 26: $2666
Year 12: $1539	Year 17: $1873	Year 22: $2279	Year 27: $2772
Year 13: $1601	Year 18: $1948	Year 23: $2370	Year 28: $2882
Year 14: $1665	Year 19: $2026	Year 24: $2465	Year 29: $2999
Year 15: $1732	Year 20: $2107	Year 25: $2563	Year 30: $3119

As expensive as renting can be, when a potential home buyer sees the "TIL" (Truth-in-Lending Disclosure), it can be a shock.

The TIL details how much they'll pay for the home over time. This number can seem enormous to buyers, creating anxiety and even cold feet when it comes to signing the escrow papers. And yet, to put the TIL in perspective, a buyer must consider how much *rent* they are expected to pay in the next 30 years... and what they'll end up with.

Taking the rental example above further, if we begin with a rent of $1,000 per month that increases 4 percent each year, the renter will wind up spending $673,019 — with absolutely nothing to show for all of their payments! In the chart below, the Truth Concepts Maximum Potential Calculator (typically used to calculate savings capability) is utilized to see how the payment and the total amount balloon over 30 years:

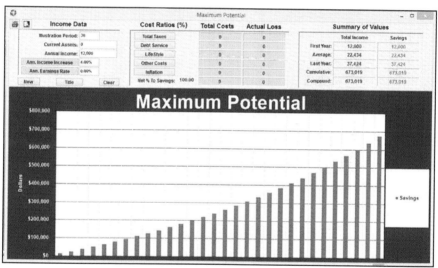

So if it will cost $673,019 to *rent* a home for 30 years, what will it cost to *buy* the home?

A home buyer who makes the leap from renting a home for $1,000 per month to purchasing a home for $200,000 at a 5 percent interest rate will see on their Truth in Lending Statement that their mortgage loan will actually cost them $386,512 in principal and interest. Plus, they'll have additional costs such as homeowner's insurance, and often mortgage insurance, worked in to the payment.

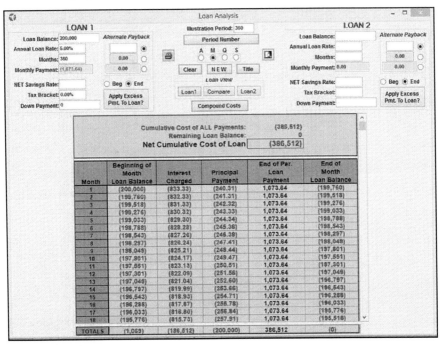

The homebuyer who was renting at $1,000 per month will see a jump in their monthly payment, perhaps of 30–40 percent, depending on the type of mortgage and the local property taxes. (The rental example of $1,000 per month and the starter home price of $200,000 are both just slightly above current national averages; in some markets, you may have to double or triple the numbers to reflect your neighborhood.)

Using the Truth Concepts Real Estate Analysis calculator to illustrate, we'll assume the buyer takes a $200,000 loan and pays $5,000 in closing costs. With estimated principal, interest, homeowner's insurance, and property taxes (which vary widely according to region), the buyer ends up paying $1,324 per month to start—over

30 percent more per month than our renter. (We included an estimated $100 per month for maintenance in the example, and additional mortgage insurance would be added to some types of loans.)

In this example, we see that the closing costs and extra expenses of buying a home produce a 15.72 percent rate of return over time. The rate of return is much higher than our estimated appreciation rate of 4 percent because of the homeowner's ability to leverage a mortgage to control an asset that is many times larger than their investment.

Some would say a renter is better off to keep renting and invest the difference (which a few do), but is that true? As rents creep up with inflation, the principal and interest portion of the homeowner's payment stays the same. After about 10 years, our renter is likely paying just as much as or more than our homeowner. There is no "difference" to invest, nor any equity being built!

In summary, renting a home beginning at $1,000 per month could cost as much as $673,019 over 30 years. At the end of that time, however, the landlord has a paid-off home and the renter has nothing.

In contrast, a homeowner might have paid approximately $622,067—that's $386,510 in principal and interest, as shown above, plus an additional estimated $235,557 in property taxes, insurance, and maintenance (assuming our starting figure of $350 and accounting for 4 percent inflation each year.)

Not only might the homeowner pay *less* than the renter over time (because the principal and interest payment remain unchanged while the renter's entire payment will keep inflating), most importantly, they own their home at the end of 30 years! At 4 percent appreciation, a $200,000 home would be worth roughly $662,700 three decades later. *The homeowner in our example comes out ahead of the renter by a whopping $715,652.*

It should no longer be a mystery why homeowners are wealthier than renters. Becoming a homeowner saves you from paying rent for decades and having nothing to show for it. It gives you a chance to keep your housing dollars in your personal economy rather than transferring them to your landlord's personal economy. And it allows you to purchase, over time, a significant asset.

Even better, as a home gains equity through appreciation and/or paying down the mortgage, you'll find yourself with greater options for the future. You'll no longer be at the mercy of landlords. And you'll have greater options for the future, such as:

- leveraging your equity to purchase a second property;
- improving your property to increase its value;
- renting out your home (or a portion of it);
- paying off your mortgage completely;
- taking a reverse mortgage;
- selling the home for a nice tax-advantaged profit. (The first

$250,000, or $500,000 for couples, is income-tax free if you have lived in the home for two of the last five years, according to current tax laws.)

Home is where the heart is. And for those who own their homes, home is also where the equity grows.

Purchasing a Home

There are many things to consider when purchasing a home. You're not just purchasing a house or a condo, you are also (typically) obtaining a mortgage and signing a long-term financial contract.

Assessing the Down Payment

With real estate, you can control a $200,000 asset using only $40,000, $10,000, or even less in some cases! That's because a mortgage allows you to use "OPM" (other people's money) when you purchase a house. Whether you put nothing down or 20 percent down, the value of the home itself does not change, only your payment and rate of return.

A surprising truth about mortgages is this: The *bigger* the down payment, the *lower* your rate of return on your investment! This is because a lower down payment allows you to increase your leverage. Real estate investors understand this, and we can demonstrate it on the Truth Concepts Real Estate Analysis calculator. If we use the same example but increase the down payment to 20 percent ($40,000), we see that our rate of return actually drops (from 15.72 percent; see Part One). We can see this in our example shown in the chart at the top of the next page.

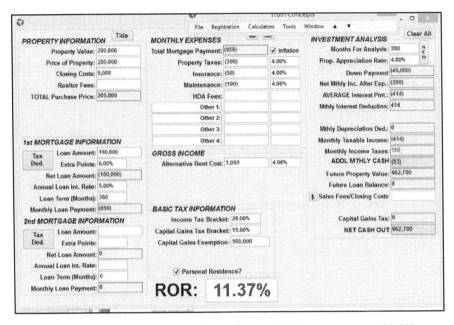

The rate of return goes *down* from 15.72 percent to 11.37 percent. It decreases because the homeowner brings more cash to the table and borrows (leverages) less. Going further using the above example, if you purchased the home outright with cash, you'd be earning only a 4 percent rate of return (minus costs) because that is the appreciation rate without any advantage of leveraging.

Many financial gurus teach home buyers to not even think of buying a home until they have a 20 percent down payment. And yet, the home you want could be appreciating out of reach while you're trying to save up your 20 percent! We recommend escaping the rent trap as soon as you are able to do so with payments you can manage.

Choosing a Mortgage

If you qualify for a zero-down VA loan (Veteran's Administration) or a nothing-down USDA loan (U.S. Department of Agriculture mortgages for more rural areas), you may want to take advantage of it. These loans have low or no mortgage insurance charges and competitive interest rates for buyers with good (or even average) credit.

Conventional loans often have the lowest interest rates, as compared to FHA (Federal Housing Administration), VA, and subprime options. The downside of conventional loans, however, is that you'll have to pay mortgage insurance unless you can make a 20 percent down payment to start.

FHA loans are easier to qualify for, credit-wise, but are unfortunately laden with fees, especially since the government got stuck guaranteeing so many failed mortgages in the Great Recession.

If you are in a rural area, USDA loans can help you obtain conventional loan rates with lower down payments and fees than typical FHA loans.

Sub-prime mortages or "hard-money loans" are still available, often from private lenders, but if you can put yourself in a position to qualify for one of the above types of loans, your interest rate and closing costs will typically be much lower.

Getting the Best Deal

When weighing your choices, you may want to ask for recommendations and check with both a brokerage and a bank. Competition and options can be good for you as a buyer. Some mortgage brokers may try to convince you that your credit won't let you qualify for the best rates, even when that's not true. Occasionally a broker can get you a better rate than a bank, or they may have access to a more appropriate type of loan that the bank (or another broker) doesn't offer. So explore a bit and get more than one quote.

There are also usually options to lower or even avoid closing costs, just as there are options to pay extra closing costs to "buy down" the interest rate. You may want to run the numbers to consider the impact over 5 or 10 years before deciding to do either, both in terms of money out of pocket and how your equity will be affected.

You'll want to make it a priority to make sure your credit score is as good as it can be prior to getting a mortgage. The difference in the mortgage interest rate you'll qualify for with a 620 FICO score and an 820 FICO score is enormous.

For example, we used a 5 percent mortgage interest rate in our calculation of a $200,000 mortgage loan, which gave us a PITI (principal, interest, taxes and insurance) payment of $1,324. However, a borrower with poor credit could end up paying as much as 10 percent interest, or $1,718 per month—a $570-per-month difference! And over 30 years, that poor-credit borrower will pay a stunning $141,840 more than the good-credit borrower will pay.

To ensure you don't overpay like that for a home, be sure to get prequalified before you start shopping, and stay within the price range you are qualified for. If necessary, clean up your credit or do what you can to raise your score. Paying down credit card balances, making all payments on time, paying off collections, and disputing negative and inaccurate information can work wonders to raise a score. And if your credit history is lacking or non-existent, work to establish positive credit through secured credit cards, department store cards, and/or an auto loan.

Finding a Home

There is much to consider when buying a home! It can be overwhelming, but when you find the right one, you'll be grateful.

Affordability. This might sound obvious, but be sure to buy a house you can afford. Too many people are "mortgage poor" because they take on a mortgage that doesn't allow them to save or take vacations, or even make needed repairs to the house! There is nothing wrong with "stretching" a bit to get yourself into a home, just make sure it is a stretch you can handle.

This is another reason why a smaller down payment can be savvy... it allows you to keep more in savings so that you have the liquidity to make needed home repairs (which are inevitable). Ample savings also allow you to handle other emergencies—or opportunities—without worrying about how to make the mortgage payment.

Many people say your home is the biggest investment you will make, but as Robert Kiyosaki points out in *Rich Dad, Poor Dad*, while you are living in it, a home is an *expense*, not an asset. You must leave yourself breathing room to save and invest apart from your mortgage.

Upside Potential. Don't buy the best home in the neighborhood. Is the home you want larger and nicer than those around it? Unless it is an excellent neighborhood, it might not be the best investment. The surrounding home values will be less and may slow the appreciation of your home or make it hard to sell. On the other hand, purchasing a smaller home and/or cosmetic fixer-upper in an excellent neighborhood gives you lots of upside potential.

Expert Assistance. Some buyers think they are going to save money by finding a home themselves instead of having a Realtor help them; however, there are risks to being a do-it-yourself home buyer. Practices and laws vary from state to state, but often the terms of a home listing with a real estate brokerage specify that if the buyer has no Realtor, the listing agent (who represents the *seller*) receives the commission that the buyer's agent would have received... *plus* the listing commission! The listing agent can collect both commissions—but they cannot represent the best interests of the buyer alone.

Imagine walking into court and finding that the opposing team's counsel is also representing YOU! You'd feel like there was no one looking out for your best interests. While real estate transactions aren't necessarily adversarial in nature, unless you are a real estate expert, you'll want someone on your side. It's not essential that this person is a Realtor, though. Experienced real estate investors, contractors, appraisers, attorneys, and other professionals can also offer great advice. Just make sure you have a person or a team who can help ensure the following:

- You are not overpaying for the home or under-estimating potential problems.
- You have the proper earnest money and mortgage pre-approval in hand.
- The contract is a legal document that protects your liability (even your earnest money) should the deal not close for some unexpected reason.
- All of the appropriate inspections are done, not just an appraisal (which is for the lender's benefit, not yours).
- Repairs are negotiated or the price renegotiated if serious issues are found—or at the very least, you have an "out" if you decide you no longer want to purchase the home after a poor inspection result.
- You receive sound advice relevant to your current market if you have to compete against other buyers.

Time to shop! Now that you have your preapproval and your team, it's time for the fun part! Make a list of what's important to you in a home... your "must haves," "would like to haves," and "can't haves" in a home. Then go house-hunting. Be open minded, listen to your gut, and always consult your advisors.

Conclusion

Thank you for investing the time and effort in your own financial education. We hope that you have enjoyed *Busting the Interest Rate Lies*, benefitted from it, and will share it with others. Books can expand your thinking and help you in "making your future bigger than your past," as Dan Sullivan suggests. Now it's time to take action by applying what you've learned.

The bottom line is this: Make sure you get the whole truth about each financial transaction. Below is a summary that can keep you from succumbing to any of the interest rate lies that are in the marketplace or the media:

Cars and Furniture: Make sure you know the all-cash price when negotiating a car purchase. Then you can work out how to finance that vehicle. As of 2015, there are some very low interest rate deals, but typically when you see zero-perecent financing, the finance company has just added the interest to the price of the car or furniture. You don't get the "cash rebate" when you finance, which must be considered.

Mortgages: Generally speaking, Prosperity Economics prefers minimum down and a 30-year fixed loan with no extra principal payments. Buy a home you can afford. Don't delay a home purchase for years simply to save a larger down payment. If you have extra money, rather than putting it toward the principal, save it where it will grow and be in your control. Obtain the best rate possible by making sure your credit is as good as it can be at the time you purchase.

Savings: Using a bank or credit union savings account, and then graduating up to using cash value of whole life, store your emergency/opportunity fund in a way that fulfills the "CLUE" philosophy—you can *Control* your money, it is *Liquid*, you can *Use* it for whatever you want with no strings attached, and you can borrow against it like *Equity*. This means the account keeps on growing while you can leverage it for dollars to help with an emergency or create an opportunity.

Investments: Look for investments that earn double digits with no loss of principal. Beware of the interest rate lie of "average." Keep looking until you find one that you are comfortable with. If you need help, contact us at the Prosperity Economics Movement for financial advisors nationwide who practice Prosperity Economics. There's no minimum required to get started, although some products do have minimums or investor qualifications.

Finally, please share this book with anyone you know who is interested in their own personal finances—high school or college students, recent graduates, or anyone who wants to gain control of their own finances and stay on the earning side of interest rates.

While Emily and Gary are fictional characters, Prosperity Economics helps real people build sustainable wealth using timeless principles, savvy strategies, and proven financial vehicles. Find out more about Prosperity Economics in the following pages, online at ProsperityPeaks.com, or by contacting the advisor who recommended this book to you. If you do not have an advisor familiar with Prosperity Economics thinking and you live in the United States, you can reach out through our website for personal help in all the areas covered in the book.

Acknowledgments

As always with books, an entire team of people help to get the manuscript across the finish line. I am always grateful there are people who have skill in areas that I don't, and I'm thrilled to have their engagement in this project. I've listed below everyone I can think of—but I'm sure I've missed a few, so my apologies. I'll keep a running list for the next book so no one gets missed!

Todd Langford for his Truth Concepts calculators and endless support.

Andrew Chapman for his publishing expertise and guidance.

Mona Kuljurgis for literally co-writing this book with me.

Kate Phillips for content editing, real estate tips, writing the home-buying section, and marketing help.

Tammi Brannan at InstinctiveLife.com for keeping me on track.

John Holzmann for his excellent feedback and suggestions on many points in the book.

The numerous financial advisors who practice Prosperity Economics for their ideas.

Todd Strobel, for co-hosting *The Prosperity Podcast* with me and his *NO BS Money Guy* work.

The entire team at P4P (from full-timers to freelancers): Jill Molitor, Theresa Sheridan, Delores Zuniga, Gabe Mendoza, Mimi Klosterman, Jeune Taylor, Carrie Putman, Terra Paley, Iman Khan, Tawny Grant, Jason Rink, and Ryan Bradshaw.

All of Todd's and my kids: Jake Langford, Jessica Langford, Robby Butler, and Kaylea Butler.

My parents, Dan and Melissa Hays, and Todd's parents, Philip and Carmen Langford.

AND Emma Dawg, our blue harlequin Great Dane (below). Oh, and the alpacas and flying squirrels, too. I'm pretty sure I couldn't have done it without them.

About the Author

Kim D. H. Butler is a leader in the Prosperity Economics Movement and an often-interviewed expert on whole life insurance and alternative investments. She has also authored: *Busting the Financial Planning Lies*, which explores the difference between "typical" financial planning and Prosperity Economics; *Busting the Retirement Lies*, a handbook for re-thinking retirement; and *Live Your Life Insurance*, a best-selling book that reveals how to use whole life insurance to enjoy greater prosperity while you're still alive!

Kim got her start in banking and then worked as a financial planner, obtaining her Series 7 and Series 65 licenses along with her financial planning certification. However, she grew disillusioned as she came to realize that the practices of typical financial planning were irrelevant, misleading, and even harmful! The projections and assumptions of typical financial planning gave clients a false sense of security, but no guaranteed results. Worst of all, the system rewarded planners when they convinced clients to put (and keep) their money at risk and under the control of others.

Driven to find a better way, Kim studied what wealthy people did and observed what worked and what didn't work in the real world. She found synergy between strategies that followed certain principles. These principles later became the 7 Principles of Prosperity™, a foundation of the Prosperity Economics Movement.

In 1999, Kim left her established company and created Partners for Prosperity, Inc., dedicated to the principles of Prosperity Economics. Rather than seeking "assets under management," the firm shows people how to build sustainable wealth by controlling and benefiting from their own assets. Partners for Prosperity, Inc. is a federally Registered Investment Advisory Firm that serves clients in all 50 states.

Kim's work as a financial advisor has been recommended by financial thought leaders and authors such as Robert Kiyosaki (*Rich Dad, Poor Dad*), Tom Dyson, publisher of the *Palm Beach Letter* investment newsletter, Tom Wheelright (*Tax-Free Wealth*), and Garret Gunderson (*Killing Sacred Cows*). Butler has also been interviewed by Robert Kiyosaki, consulted by the *Palm Beach Letter*, appeared on the popular "Real Estate Guys" radio show, and was featured in several programs hosted by financial services expert Steve Savant, who called her "a Joan of Arc crusader separating financial fact from fiction." Kim also co-hosts The Prosperity Podcast on iTunes.

Butler is a mentor to many as an associate coach for Strategic Coach and through Truth Training and The Summit for Prosperity Economics Advisors, events that Kim facilitates along with her husband, Todd Langford of Truth Concepts software.

Mona Kuljurgis is a writer and editor living near Washington, D.C. She thanks Kim Butler for revealing to her, via this and other projects, the whole truth about her money.

About the Prosperity Economics Movement

Before the rise of qualified retirement plans, the ever-present 401(k), and the financial planning industry, people built wealth with diligence and common-sense strategies. Investors created wealth through building equity and ownership in properties, businesses, and participating (dividend-paying) whole life insurance. Only a few dabbled in Wall Street stocks, or built "portfolios" on paper.

Wealthy people, in fact, have never stopped practicing what we call "Prosperity Economics."

Today, the common investor is steered away from traditional wealth-building methods. Instead, they are confronted with a confusing labyrinth of funds, rates and complex financial instruments of questionable value. Mutual funds have become so complex that even the people who sell them can't explain them, nor predict when investors are about to lose money. Worse yet, over 30 percent of the average investor's wealth is drained away in fees to a financial industry rife with conflicts of interest.

Prosperity Economics Movement (PEM) is a rediscovery of the traditional simple and trusted ways to grow and protect your money. It was started to provide American investors an alternative to "typical" financial planning, showing us how to control our own wealth instead of delegating our financial futures to corporations and the government.

In Prosperity Economics, wealth isn't measured by how much money you have, but by how much *freedom* you have with your money. The focus is on cash flow rather than net worth. Liquidity, control, and safety are valued over uncertain hopes of a high rate of return. (See the diagram on the next page for some key differences between Prosperity Economics and "typical" financial planning.)

Prosperity Economics Movement is actually comprised of smaller movements that represent alternatives to a financial planning industry we believe has gone off course. You may have heard of The Infinite Banking Concept, Private or Family Banking, Rich Dad Strategies, Circle of Wealth, or Bank on Yourself. Advisors and agents within the movement may use different language and even suggest different financial strategies, but they honor a common set of principles, such as the 7 Principles of Prosperity articulated by Kim Butler.

Typical financial planning is better than nothing, and will get you partway up the hill, but we want to show you how to reach the "peaks" of prosperity. Prosperity Economics shows you how to grow your wealth safely and reliably, with maximum financial flexibility and cash flow. To find out more about Prosperity Economics and PEM, we invite you to explore our website at ProsperityPeaks.com.

Financial Planning versus	**Prosperity Economics**™
Meets needs and goals only	Pursues wants and dreams
Minimizes requirements	Optimizes opportunities
Product oriented (only what you buy)	Strategy oriented (what you do)
Rate of return focused	Opportunity cost recovery focused
Institutions control your money	You control your money
Micro (vacuum) based	Macro (big picture) based
Net worth is measurement	Cash flow is measurement
Retirement oriented	Abundant/Freedom oriented
Lives only on interest	Spends and replaces principal
Money stays still	Money moves
Dollars do only one job	Dollars do many jobs
Professional planner is the expert	You are empowered

Work with a Prosperity Economics Advisor

If you don't like your cash sitting at 1 percent—taxable—and you want your investment to grow without the roller-coaster ride of the market, we can help. To explore alternative financial strategies that put you in the driver's seat, we invite you to have a no-cost, no-obligation conversation with a Prosperity Economics Advisor. Simply email Welcome@ProsperityPeaks.com to set an appointment with Kim Butler or one of her hand-picked advisors.

We will find out more about you and your situation, and evaluate how your money might work harder without subjecting it to risk, unnecessary taxation, and never-ending fees. We'll likely suggest proven alternative approaches to "financial planning as usual," and we can even refer you to a truly effective debt solution if needed. We have found these strategies through experience, and they have worked well for our clients.

The three main areas of interest for most people are: cash storage, asset growth, and income. We help clients implement alternative strategies for each of these desires. Our cash strategy grows cash many times faster than typical bank CD rates, while deferring taxes and offering other benefits. Our stock market alternative (especially effective for accredited investors) has an excellent track record with our clients and is not affected by stock market conditions, interest rates, or politics. We can even suggest alternatives to bonds or annuities for cash flow that offer more attractive rates without requiring a long-term surrender of assets.

Simply send an email to Welcome@ProsperityPeaks.com to get started or find out more.

In the meantime, we invite you to explore ProsperityPeaks.com, a website dedicated to Prosperity Economics. And as special thank-you for purchasing this book, readers can download a free 60-page ebook, *Financial Planning Has FAILED*. In this landmark book, Kim Butler and Kate Phillips tell it like it is about the financial industry and illustrate how Prosperity Economics provides real solutions for anyone who wishes to build wealth without Wall Street risks and worries.

Go to ProsperityPeaks.com/financial and get your copy today.

Book a Prosperity Economics Speaker for Your Next Event!

For general audiences

Throughout the country, Prosperity Economics spokespersons are available to speak about the differences between typical financial planning and Prosperity Economics, along with related financial topics.

Are you looking for a particular subject area? Perhaps your audience would like to learn:

- Retirement plan realities—why qualified plans don't perform as illustrated
- How to save without the risks and roller coaster of the stock market
- Qualified plan alternatives that can significantly reduce future taxes
- The impact of inflation and the danger of retiring too soon
- Saving enough? Why most of us need to save more!
- Financial Planning versus Prosperity Economics

For advisors

Author **Kim Butler** and Truth Concepts founder **Todd Langford** are available to speak to advisors or agents about Prosperity Economics, including a Truth Concepts demo that uses calculators and tools to illustrate some of the distinctions of Prosperity Economics. (Truth Concepts is financial software dedicated to telling the whole truth about money. It's built for advisors yet available to anyone at TruthConcepts.com.)

This 2–3 hour presentation is a fascinating eye-opener about various financial philosophies and concepts, and how to talk about and illustrate various financial strategies with clients. Contact Kim@Partners4Prosperity.com for details.

Truth Training

Langford and Butler also conduct seminars several times a year for advisors (anyone is welcome) on using Truth Concepts software. Purchase of the software is not necessary, any advisor can benefit, and some find it so beneficial they return again and again! For more information, go to TruthConcepts.com.

The Prosperity Economics Movement is a not-for-profit organization comprising financial experts who practice Prosperity Economics and individuals who would like to learn how to apply the principles of Prosperity Economics to improve their lives. This book is part of a growing body of information that will support the organization and its members.

To learn more or buy your own copy of this book, go to:
www.ProsperityPeaks.com

66984409R00091

Made in the USA
Charleston, SC
04 February 2017